How to be a Kenyan

WAHOME MUTAHI

KENWAY PUBLICATIONS
Nairobi • Kampala • Dar es Salaam

Published by Kenway Publications
a subsidiary of
East African Educational Publishers Ltd.
Brick Court, Mpaka Road/Woodvale Grove, Westlands
P.O. Box 45314, Nairobi

East African Educational Publishers Ltd.
Pioneer House, Jinja Road
P.O. Box 11542, Kampala

Ujuzi Educational Publishers Ltd.
P.O. Box 31647, Dar es Salaam

ISBN 9966 46 562 6

Edited by
David Round-Turner

Printed in Kenya by English Press Ltd.
Enterprise Road, P.O. Box 30127, Nairobi

Contents

Contents

Is it imported?

I grew up under the inspiration of my rural neighbour and would have taken his former career if the circumstances had allowed. The man was the retired cook of one Mr Hall, a settler farmer in colonial Kenya. It looked as if Mr Hall had given him a new sound which in my innocence I, too, wanted to own.

When he escorted me home after yet another evening of why and when he did this and that or did not do it because that is not how Mr Hall taught him, he would call my attention to the way he was holding the torch.

He would tell me, "This is the right way to hold the torch. Even Mr Hall appreciated it when I held the torch thus. He was a man who could not stand nonsense and I always held the torch like this because that is the way he liked it and so it is the right one."

That neighbour had the distinction of owning what was called a *"mzungu* cow" – a breed imported from Europe. Whenever I came to see the neighbour, he complimented me for having acquired a *mzungu* haircut, a simple cut with short hair on the back and sides. He prided himself over keeping time like a *mzungu* and when he ate a good meal, he said he had eaten like a *mzungu*.

The only *mzungu* I knew then was the local parish priest and there were a few things that made me think that if he was like Mr Hall, then my neighbour had learned a number of great things from him. Having been used to a pit latrine outside the house, I thought the priest was so different from us that he did not go to the toilet. I could not imagine a lavatory inside a house.

My neighbour and the priest have since died but not the expressions, "he keeps time like a *mzungu*" and "my *mzungu* has not paid me my wages." In reference to one's African boss, he is your *mzungu* meaning boss, since at one time only a *mzungu* provided employment.

But the word *mzungu* – to mean something good – is almost gone except in my villlage. It now sounds more intelligent to say, "That is a nice shirt you are wearing. Is it imported?" You nod effusively if the shirt bears a label indicating it was made in Europe or America. Perhaps that shirt was made in Nairobi's

1

industrial area and so was the label that says it was imported from London. It is all part of the innovation by manufacturers to satisfy those who are ready to pay a price for an item when the label says that it has been made anywhere other than in Kenya.

That is why a Kenyan will go to London and buy a suit made in Kenya and available in Nairobi at twice its local price. The pain of paying dearly is compensated by the pride in saying, "I bought this suit in London."

In those days when my neighbour was trying to turn me into a cook for a white man, going abroad for studies was an issue that concerned the entire clan and sometimes the whole village, not just because some money had to be raised by the community for what was invariably called "further studies," but also for fear of the student bringing home unpopular imports.

One such "import" was a white wife. There were the village hardliners who believed that a wife who could not till land was not worth the bride price and so any of the clan's sons going to study abroad was warned that he was expected to bring back such imports as university degrees and not a wife.

The advice was not always taken and when such a student returned home with a degree and a white wife, the new wife was not scalded with water by the elders who were angry that they had been defied. In many instances the man got such looks that said, "Our son is great. He went to the land of the white people and not only got their education but also a wife from their people."

Such an "import" is still considered an achievement and so is getting education abroad, even if it is from a village university.

If I cannot get that imported thing in the shops, I can always have the foreign association with what I buy locally. What, with the expatriates around leaving for their countries or to other countries where their "expert" services are needed!

Some years ago, all that I needed to inspire me to buy that car at the required price without complaining was to read it advertised thus: "Peugeot car for sale. European owned".

I don't remember whether it was because of local lobbying against subtle racism in such advertisements or a sudden illumi-

2

mination, but such advertisements in the newspapers are no more. In their place are others that mean the same, the most popular one being, "car for sale, expatriate leaving".

"I bought it from an expatriate"

The equation is simple: Expatriate means a white person and white person equals good. Such an equation inspires such talk as, "I bought it from an expatriate and you know how careful expatriates are with their cars".

Having grown up under the former employee of Mr Hall, I am not surprised that I find myself saying, "There were three people and one European in the hotel," implying that the three Africans are different from the European. I am not alone in making that kind of racial equation. It is something I also hear from other people.

3

"Flied lice"

"Just you wait; you will see me." Translation: "I will teach you a lesson." Very mild sounding, but it could very well be a real death threat.

I will be the last one to take it lightly. Known to put on a tough face, I will rant at my adversary, "Just you dare, you... You are very cow."

That's English alright with much help from my mother tongue which I share with my adversary. It comes to my aid when I speak English and I get quite well understood...well, by Kenyans because the majority think in their mother tongues and then put the thoughts in English as they speak.

That is why I will never eat porridge and will happily drink it. I will never ask my wife to make tea for me but she will gladly "cook" it for me to "drink" and not to "take" it. Don't tell me that I am being "silly" by letting out the secrets of how I speak because I will take that to mean that I am the daftest person on earth since Adam was duped by his wife. If you do so, I will remember that insult with utmost disgust till I die.

When new technology was introduced in our newspaper offices, many of us hurried back from the butcheries where we were "measuring" our kilos of mid-day roasts. There were no tape measures and all but, all we had asked the butcher to do was put some cuts on the scales to make the weight of what we wanted for our lunch.

Back in the office, we "saw with our mouths" when we looked at the new technology. Our eyes did not move to the location of our mouths. All that happened was that our eyes popped out in wonder as widely as mouths that were agape. Later on, a cub reporter hurried into the newsroom with the "burning" news that two cars had collided in the unusual fashion of "buttock-to-buttock".

Back at home, I was trying to tell my wife about the new technology in the office that would help us make our competitors "see dust" – come last – when she told me to "hold the news" since she wanted to go to the kitchen and make the food "catch fire". She had no intentions of setting the pot and its contents on fire and all she wanted to do was warm the food. I ate and when I thanked her for making me "fed up", she was not offended. She was happy to have done the duty of making her husband well-fed.

In a newspaper office, one can get fed up by a rural correspondent filing a story by a telephone connection that sounds as if it is on the moon. Such a correspondent is usually given a pep talk on how to be audible: "You are speaking too slowly, man. I can hardly hear you." This is not a cue to ask the correspondent to speak more words per minute but to remind him that the line is so faint that he should raise his volume.

I take two days off from the office and when I return, there is such pumping of hands that one gets the impression that I have just risen from the dead, an impression that is further reinforced when somebody says, "W.M., you are really lost. How have you been?" It is another way of saying, "How was your weekend."

I have to work in a newspaper office where correspondents speak "slowly" because I have yet to "fall on things", that is , "to cross the valley of poverty". This also means that it cannot be said that "W.M. has a few things here and there". Since I don't have any of those labels, the clear implication is that I am simply a poor wage earner.

The modesty that makes a man of property be described as one who "owns a few things here and there" is what might mislead you if a Kenyan tells you that he has got "something small on the fire" and invites you to come along and "just have a piece". That translates to, "I have a kilo of meat roasting at Karanja's butchery. Let us go and make a meal of it."

Being the beneficiary of such generosity, it is quite in order for you to "return the hand". What a better way than to invite your benefactor for a drink in the evening, for returning the hand is reciprocating generosity.

The invitation to "return the hand" is announced with modesty that matches the earlier offer for lunch. It is extended with the words, "Chief, let us go and have one after work. I have got a pound in my pocket." That means, "I have two or so thousand shillings that I want to spend so let us go and get drunk."

It might not be the kind of evening you would want to have – if like my fellow compatriot from Central Province, you had lunch that consisted of such specialities as "flied lice". I come from a place where we banished "Rs" and in their place found a comfortable place for "Ls" and where "Ns" and "Ms" sneak into conversation when they should be absent. Naturally, I "Ngo home when I chund be washing footmball", because "sh" becomes "ch" after which I shall have a packet of "ships" sold for a few "chirings".

5

English is the official language, but that was not a good enough reason for my English teacher to make me and those who found intimacy with that language difficult; to carry a block of wood inscribed, "I am a fool" round the neck for speaking one of "those native languages." The teacher spoke what he called vocabulary, a language we did not understand, in his effort to make us adopt the tongue of the white school inspector who impressed us more with his array of pens of all colours stuck in his stockings below his short khaki pants than with the English which, as we said, "he spoke through the nose".

When the teacher got into a fit of anger because one of us had dared speak anything that sounded remotely like English, he spoke in a language similar to English. He threatened to deal with us "perpendicularly and horizontally". He would look at such an offender like "a rotten piece of horticulture" and he claimed that his bicycle "descended the hill to the school at great locomotion".

Kiswahili is the national language and for reasons other than to sound official and national, my children speak the two languages at the same time. They call the language "sheng", which is a curious hybrid of the two languages. The language is spoken to keep father and mother out of the conversation because the language has no dictionary or formal classes and is spoken almost exclusively by the young generation that knows the chemistry of making words and mixing them.

So I am sitting there and my son is telling his friend, without any hint of conspiracy: "Aise Joe, jana niliheight to death tukiwa na yule dame wa mine. Usha muspy yule dame, yani yule chick wa akina Mike. Yeye ni kiboko to death, ama? We heighted a major one. Tulistay mpaka masides ya midnight. Zile books sijazicheck na mahomework nimeyasare."

I have a lot of confidence in my son and I have convinced myself that he has a great future ahead of him. Although he wears a haircut that makes him look as if I picked him from a US ghetto, prefers shoes that look like stilts and walks as if his heels are on fire, I still think that he will take after me and read hard to make a career for himself.

So when the young man is talking to his friend in that language, which to me might as well be something from Outer Mongolia, I string a few words from the conversation and imagine that he is telling his friend, "Yesterday I studied until I nearly died. I did not

6

read any of that spy stuff that won't make me get anywhere as Mike does. I read up to midnight and finished my homework."

The translation of what he says is of course what would explain why he has been demanding clothes that make him look as if he is a rock star. It translates: "Pal, last night I had a good time with my girl-friend. You know her of course. She is Mike's sister and she is quite a beauty as you know. We drank until midnight and I have not touched that boring homework that was given at school."

Harambee!

Bank managers are not everybody's friends. Even when they can listen sympathetically to a loan application, the interest they charge is not friendly. But who said banks are the only source of money? Who said that one must pay when he cannot pay?

There are friendlier ways of getting that car needing an engine overhaul back on the road. One of them is suddenly remembering that you were born on a day you cannot specifically recall. The fact that you have a birthday is all that matters, not the fact that you cannot remember whether you are a Scorpio or a Capricorn.

Armed with the knowledge that you were born on a day in the past, you print cards that announce that on such and such a day you have the pleasure of inviting your friends to your birthday party. The unwritten message in the invitation card, which most people who receive the cards know is that when a person is celebrating age, he does not fete friends; he is feted.

So as soon as the cards have been dispatched for the birthday party on that day on which you were not born, you sit and wait for goodwill because the cards are sent out selectively. They go out to both friends and enemies who are more likely to dig into their pockets rather than into that dish of meat that is sparingly passed around during the party.

It is all in the spirit of harambee or self-help which, in this case, means helping yourself to the generosity of friends.

You don't have to feel guilty about it since harambee is a national motto to help self and group. On the day of the party, all is ready, especially that table near the entrance bearing the sign, "gifts here". The sign has to be placed so invitingly that anybody entering will feel guilty passing by the table without giving something to congratulate you for reaching a certain age.

You make it convenient for everybody to give something by having a batch of empty envelopes on the gifts table and making sure that the person manning that important station has a personality that can talk money out of the guests' pockets.

A charming lady always does the trick, particularly with men as few men are likely to let down a beauty stretching an empty envelope towards them.

The general idea is to discourage wrapped gifts for while the gift wrappings may be pretty, what they conceal might not be worth the piece of meat that guest will eat. A person celebrating a birthday, even when he does not know when he was born, does not like being bundled with tin cups presented under the cover of tinsel wrapping. He would rather receive something inside a khaki envelope handed over at the door.

Such a person tries to make everybody except himself feel guilty about being mean on that day. He will want you to understand that he is not Jesus who fed a crowd with five loaves of bread and that you should, therefore, be satisfied with the pieces of bread that are being selectively passed around.

The host achieves the effect of spreading guilt among those guests who have not picked the khaki envelopes and stuffed them with currency notes by sitting at the head of the high table. He is most likely festooned with a paper garland and in many ways is like a medieval chief receiving his subjects.

This is so because after each guest receives a khaki envelope and puts something in it, he goes to hand it over to the host. It is excessively bad manners not to be seen handing over your envelope to the host to wish him a happy birthday and a prosperous future.

It will most likely be a prosperous immediate future because at the end of the evening he will be richer by many khaki envelopes loaded with currency notes, for nobody would dare put coins in them. The harambee might be so successful that the man will be tempted to organise another function on similar lines, most likely to mark his wedding anniversary even though he has never had a church wedding.

Sometimes such prosperity comes to you in a harambee even when you have not invited it directly. My first goat was such a benefit acquired at a harambee. The committee of the Presbyterian Church in my village had the misguided conception that since my byline was prominent in the newspaper I worked for, it reflected my network of rich friends, who would give me money to take to the harambee they had arranged to raise money to buy pews.

I was to be the guest of honour because a harambee for a public project must have one such person who is supposed to bring in loads of money in his pocket and in the pockets of those friends who have come to "escort him", as it is said of those who accompany the guest of honour.

9

I lost many friends because, as it often happens when you are the guest of honour, you are given funds collection receipts in form of booklets.

So I meet a friend and because I want to build a good name during that harambee by raising as much money as possible, at the risk of annoying my Member of Parliament who thinks he has the prerogative of raising record amounts, I fish out the harambee booklet from my pocket.

There are quite a number of receipts that have been filled in with names of donors and their pledges although I have not received any money from them. I shall have to chase the pledgers later.

I open the booklet and leaf through it pretending that I cannot get the receipt where I will enter the amount that I expect my friend to pledge. The truth is that I want him to see that those who have pledged money before him are not mean and that he should therefore match their amounts if not promise to give more.

The friend looks at me as if I work for the income tax department but all the same scribbles an amount on the receipt, yet another pledge that I have to chase when the harambee date approaches.

Collecting money from such pledges is not easy as the pledgers are either not available or have suddenly lost a distant relative and cannot pay.

Of course, the folks back home did not understand that I was dealing with defaulters in the city. When the day of the harambee came, they expected me to prove their assumption that I am an illustrious son of the village right. That is a thought they emphasise by having choirs and traditional dancing groups perform for you when you are the guest of honour. In my case they sang about "W.M., the son of a great woman, who had gone to school, read all the books that are there to be read, got a job and has now come to bring development to his people."

As the praise singing went on, trays of food landed on the high table where I was sitting with the church committee members. There was plenty of goat meat, chicken and rice, which surprised me because I knew that rice is such a rare commodity in my mother's kitchen and the kitchens of other villagers that it was only eaten on special occasions. I was also sure that the goat meat had not been bought from a butchery, and that goats must have been slaughtered for the occasion.

10

As the church committee members and I washed our hands after the sumptuous meal, the choirs and traditional dancers who had not yet exhausted praise songs for the "great son of the soil" retired to feed on soda and pieces of dry bread. It is all part of protocol on such occasions for the guest of honour and the committee organising the harambee to be fed properly so that they can "have the saliva to call for donations from the people". Apparently, the saliva expended by the choir members and traditional dancers can be easily restored by drinking soda and eating a dry piece of bread.

Having failed to collect most of the pledges from my friends, I could not challenge the fund-raising records of my Member of Parliament. Since I have no aspirations for political power, I also did not take a loan to impress the people that I am "development conscious" by "pouring" it out at the harambee meeting. We did not meet the Shs 30,000 target because I gave five thousand and the local people raised seven thousand. They expected me to bring Shs 23,000 as that is what an illustrious son of the village is expected to do as he works in the "city of many lights", as my aunt will want to say when she talks about Nairobi, the place where money is never in short supply.

Even having so miserably failed to raise the targeted amount, I was not bid farewell with angry stares, for you never do that to a guest of honour. As behoves protocol, the choirs and teams of the traditional dancers were summoned back to the field to "thank the guest of honour for performing his duties well" by singing more praise songs. That was not enough though to thank a man who had come all the way from the city to "bring development". I had to be thanked with something more substantial than songs.

So the chairman of the church committee stood tall before the microphone and after saying how important it was for parents to educate their children so that they could become "like W.M." and be "development conscious", he looked in the distance and said, "though we may be poor, we are not mean."

That seemed to be a signal to a goat to bleat in the distance, behind the crowd that ringed the dais. The goat bleated again and the cause of such insistent noise from the animal became clear in a short while when I saw a young man pulling a goat by its leash and another one pushing the reluctant animal towards the dais. No sooner was it at my feet than the chairman of the committee said, pointing at the goat,

11

"This small goat is for you to take back to the city for your soup so that you may come here much more often to bring us development."

I looked at the "small animal" which was supposed to provide soup and wondered how I was going to take it back to the city in my small saloon car. The "small" animal was a billy goat reaching me to the waist. It had a beard as generous as its horns and was big enough to feed a family of ten for weeks. Yet according to the chairman, I was expected to "make a small meal of soup so that I could find energy to return to the village".

MEEE....

The answer as to how to carry the animal was provided by the two youths who trussed the goat into a sack and squeezed it into the boot of my car.

I later learnt that the church committee did not buy the pews. They could not because Barnabas, the local shopkeeper, was threatening to burn the local church if he was not paid for the rice that was taken on credit to feed the guest of honour and the church committee.

Josiah, the owner of the goat that had been given to me had forgotten his Christian spirit of tolerance and was threatening to murder the chairman of the church committee if he was not paid for the animal. The local auctioneer was threatening to auction the entire church committee and their families if he was not paid his fee for the hire of his public address system.

My harambee had left a lot of bad will because books would not balance. The people in the village had expected me to raise more than the targeted amount so that they could use the excess amount to pay for the debts incurred. They later thought it wise to have an empty house of God rather than the chairman dead at the hands of Josiah, reformed sinner.

That has not saved me from other harambees where I make pledges and sometimes pay cash. Soon it will be difficult not to be confronted by a Kenyan wanting a cash contribution for a harambee to buy a carburettor for his pastor's car, to help a friend stage a church wedding, take a body from Nairobi back home for burial, help the son of a real estate tycoon go to a prestigious university abroad, or help out a man who wants to complete his bank loan when he invites me to the birthday party of his son who was born six months ago.

Hallo, hallo...

A telephone booth has many uses, one of which is to offer a good target for vandals and other people who want to vent their anger on something. There is something about those red telephone booths that invites stones on their glass panes. There is something about their doors that makes them susceptible to being slammed angrily.

There is something that makes the telephone sets inside the booths so attractive that they are ripped off when there is nobody looking. Perhaps it has something to do with the fact that sometimes, even when the equipment is in place, it is not working. There is a chance that some of those telephone sets are ripped off by angry callers who have been ripped off by public telephone sets that just swallow money without the call going through.

That is why those booths are often just pieces of decoration dotting the city as either the handset has been ripped off or the thing is there but not working at all. It is easy to tell a booth that is suffering from either affliction; there is no queue in front of it.

The easiest way of locating a functional telephone booth is to look for a public telephone service queue. The queue more or less tells you that the telephone in that particular booth is working. But keep your fingers crossed until you actually make the call because misfortune could strike any time. It could be that that particular person in the booth has been there for quite a while and does not know how to use the telephone, and although he has placed money in the coin slot and is holding the receiver against his ear, the telephone is dead.

That kind of person will often be very theatrical. With the earpiece as close as it can be to the ear, he or she will shout interminably "Hallo! Hallo!" into the mouth piece. The other end will either be dead or will produce unpleasant and unintelligible sounds. The telephone user will hit the telephone rest thrice in succession, smack the coin box in an apparent effort to make the coins drop into it. Once again, he will shout interminable "hallos" and most likely repeat the procedure of hitting the telephone armrest and the coin box.

Meanwhile a queue will have formed at the telephone booth and silent curses will be made under the breath of those who think that the telephone is working. The queue will not melt as soon as the second person goes into the booth and walks out after announcing that it is out of order. A third, fourth and fifth person will enter the booth and each will try to prove the second person who went in and said that the thing was not working wrong by trying to call three times without success.

The queue will then melt only to form later as soon as somebody enters the same booth and stays for three to five minutes trying to make a telephone call.

Annoyed by such a telephone that does not work, you could get even by slamming the door of the booth and by calling the Kenya Posts people something nasty under your breath, punishment that you cannot apply with equal measure to other telephone users who forget where they are once they are inside that booth and the telephone is working.

Torture by the telephone starts after you have joined a queue now that you have seen the person inside the booth doing much more than just saying "hallo, hallo" into the mouthpiece. Finally you see hope because there are two people ahead of you.

The one ahead enters and does not put any money in the coin slot, but he is talking on the telephone. He replaces it on its rest and folds his arms. The girl infront of you opens the door and asks him what is wrong. He says with confidence that there is nothing wrong and shuts the door. He folds his arms once again and the telephone hand set continues resting in its place.

After ten minutes, it rings and he grabs it as if he is afraid that somebody else will snatch it.

"Hallo!...Hallo!..." he shouts as if he is talking to somebody in the bowels of the earth. Hallo!...Hallo! is that North Horr number twenty six...but there was...yes, twenty six... North Horr, yes." He replaces the receiver and folds his arms once again and we wait patiently for it to ring again, for it is clear now that he is making an operator-assisted call.

Another ten minutes and the telephone does not ring. The caller picks up the receiver, gives it a bad look and calls the operator once again. Apparently the operator is not in a mood to respond to "Hallo! Operator!...Hallo, is that the operator? Operator... Hallo, operator..." The caller gives up, walks out and most likely slams the door of the booth.

The girl ahead of you gets inside. She places her handbag on the directory rack which is vacant because public telephone directories find better use wrapping things in shops. She opens her bag and out

15

comes a pocket diary which she thumbs through without any hurry. After finding the number that she wants to call, she places the diary on top of the telephone and opens her bag once again and takes out coins.

You think that she is going to make a long distance telephone call because she has put a row of coins in the money slot. She however calls a city number. The appropriate coins fall into place but the amount is still enough to make a long distance call. "Hallo," she says enthusiastically. "Is that double four, six, double zero...Kamau and Associates Battery Manufacturers... hallo...hallo....is that...Wrong number did you say?"

She replaces the receiver with a bang and thumbs through her diary once again. She comes to an entry and then dials. The receiver stays clutched to her cheek for about a minute without any conversation going on. She replaces the receiver and just when you are about to sigh with relief thinking that she will get out, she goes back to the diary and thumbs through it again.

You decide to leave but then you realise that will mean queuing once again behind another telephone booth, for you must make that call. You watch the girl as she dials again. This time the call goes through quickly and you praise yourself inwardly for your patience.

The girl is looking as thoroughly relaxed as if she is in her sitting room. She opens the door slightly as she fans her face as if to say that she needs some fresh air. That means that you can hear what she is saying.

Although the conversation is meant for her and the Jane at the other end, you will be forced to listen in as the door is ajar.

"Is that Jane?...Oh Jane, how is job...Me?...I decided to skip it today...The boss? Told him that I have malaria (chuckle, chuckle, giggle, giggle then loud laughter)...Not really, just the case of a bad hangover...I had one too many with Jim...yes, that bore...I only stand him because he can take a girl to a nice place. Otherwise I cannot stand him talk about the weather and railway engines...yeah, we went places...with two of his friends...Much more entertaining guys...really cool guys...(chuckle, chuckle, giggle, giggle)."

There are giggles behind you from people who are amused but, you are neither amused by the girl in the booth nor those finding her conversation packed with comedy. Neither the murderous look on your face nor the amusement of those in the queue bothers the girl.

She has a good listener in Jane at the other end and enough coins for the moment for public confession of vices.

She is now almost doing a dancing act as she says, "To be honest I would not mind the other guys...Introduce you to one of them? Sure, any time but you have your guy...What? Split with him? My, My! I knew it was coming...the way you looked bored to death when I last saw you together...How about next Saturday...No problem...You know me and those things..."

"Tell you what! I am running out of coins and I haven't told you that I met Christine this morning...I could not believe it. I don't know how to put it....It is unbelievable...A third one in three years...Yes, she is heavy...Yes and..."

At that moment, the last shilling falls into place and the caller tells Jane, "Just a minute..." She pokes her head out and asks, as if she is just enquiring what hour it is, "Anybody got some loose coins? I need some change." She gets angry stares even from those who were amused by her conversation earlier on. She goes back to her conversation and as soon as she says "Hallo Jane," the telephone is disconnected. She walks out of the booth in a rage against people who are so inconsiderate as not to give her change to continue with her call.

You might consider that conversation more tolerable than waiting to call while inside the booth, is a man with a voice that sounds like a bomber. That voice is booming through the closed door of the booth as he says: "Hallo! Is that Naivasha Saw Mills? Naivasha! Hallo! Hallo! Naivasha! Is that John Kimeu? Kimeu! Kimeu! Can you hear me? ...I can hear you very well, God be praised!

"How is the saw mill...Good, did you say?...Then God be praised...God is still with us here. He has been very good to me...Hallo!... I wanted to tell you that...Hallo!... Yes, now I can hear you well...I wanted to tell you that we shall be coming to...Kimeu, are you still there?

"I wanted to tell you that we...That is my wife and I...Yes, your sister in Christ...We shall come to Naivasha on Sunday!... To attend the big Christian rally there! Where the visiting white preacher will be..."

Should you face that, which is likely, you will be right to judge the telephone an instrument of torture rather than communication.

How to get lost

"What you do is first of all take this road on which we are standing . . . ."

I hated the air hostess throughout the flight because I thought she could not have found a better insult to hurl at a passenger who had paid his fare to London.

I had asked her where my seat was, and she said, without even looking at the direction in which I was supposed to sit, "Three seats down the aisle, sir. You cannot miss it." I could not understand how she could say I could not miss my seat when I had already missed it. At the same time, "three seats down the aisle" sounded like all way down to the cockpit as this was my first flight.

In London, the first time I asked for directions, the Londoner said, mouth half-closed: "Three blocks up the street and then turn left." If the man thought that he had told me words that were going to work the kind of miracle that Jesus Christ performed on the daughter of the

Roman centurion who was miles away when he said, "Go away, thy faith hath healed thee," he was wrong.

His instructions confused me even more as the only blocks we know in Nairobi are for construction and not the buildings themselves. I stood transfixed on the spot and sure that the first man was in too much of a hurry to tell me in more graphic detail the location of where I wanted to go, I stopped another person, this time a woman trusting in the patience of the female sex.

"Three blocks up the street and then turn left," she said , through her pouting mouth. It looked to me as if she feared words would break if she opened her mouth wider. Once again the words sounded as if they meant, "The hell if you don't know where you are going, what are you doing in London?"

I thought I was still in Kenya where telling the way is telling a story, for no detail, however small, should be lost. I would love to meet that man who told me "three blocks up the street" when he is lost in my home village. I have no doubt that he would be as confused as I was in his home city if I told him how to get to Karatina town.

"So you want to go to Karatina, eh," I would begin, rubbing my hands together as if I was by the fireside telling a folktale.

"What you do is first of all take this road on which we are standing and head towards that way." At that moment I would stretch my hand in the direction that I mean. After a dramatic pause, I would continue:

"You move and move until you come to a stream called Kamahuri. That is where I take my cows to drink water and if by any chance you see a small boy dressed in a green shirt herding five cows, tell him that he is taking too long at the river.

"Cross the bridge and climb the hill that you will meet. Since it is not raining, that hill should not be a problem but I tell you, *aiii*! when it rains, that hill is big trouble. It is such big trouble that even the chief's Landrover finds it difficult to climb it.

"Since your car will manage the hill, you will then see two blue gum trees as the road levels. Ignore them and just go on. After some driving, you will see a red-roofed house which belongs to Teacher John. That one is a hard-working person if you ask me, a man who has shown people what development is all about. After you have passed his house, just keep on driving and you will see another two trees but this time they are not of the blue gum type. They are cedar. Pass them.

19

"Drive on and on and if you look carefully, you will see a small path on your right. Pretend that you have not seen it and just go on. Then even if you don't look very hard, you will see another road on the left. Get ready to branch onto that one.

"Once you have done so, beware of women going to the market as today is market day at Karatina. There is something about women who are carrying loads on their backs on their way to the market; even if the sky is falling down, they cannot hear, so you must honk very loudly when you see them.

"Although you will see those women, don't think that you have arrived at Karatina. Just drive on without looking left or right because there is nowhere that you are going to turn now. Drive and drive until you see the iron sheets of Karatina shops. I am sure that you will find your way very easily. By the way, my son who has taken cattle to water wanted to go to Karatina but since he is still away, you cannot give him a lift."

Give or take a detail, that is what that Londoner will hear and will perhaps know the kind of confusion that he caused me with his "Three blocks up the street".

A journey of "three blocks" is of course faster than one that seems to start the moment it is supposed to end.

A story whose veracity I cannot vouch for is told of an ethnic group where a journey to the moon is *"no vaa"* meaning, "take a few steps and you are there."

So you meet a Mkamba, a person from that ethnic group, and as you accompany him on the journey, you ask after the first kilometre, "How far is it from here to Karatina?" You get the answer, cut and dry, *"No vaa."*

An hour later after crossing rivers and going up hills, which is certainly not the kind of distance that you can describe as three blocks up the street, you ask, "How far now" and you are told with finality, *"No vaa!"*

Another hour later, feet blistered and knees weak, you ask how far you are and you are told *"no vaa." "No vaa"* ends only when you get to your destination.

Some tea for the boss

When I worked in the civil service as a district officer, I considered myself a somewhat important personality. After all, being a public administrator, songs were sang in my praise during public rallies and people stood when I passed by. It was only later that I discovered that the singing and the standing was just a show for my messenger who not only wielded more power but also commanded real authority.

The fellow had more powers of appointment and disappointment than his boss by virtue of the simple fact that he had a desk where people who wanted to see me on official business reported. His powers lay in the fact that you had to pass through his hands before you saw me. He made the fact of seeing the boss such an issue that he naturally became a bigger authority.

He wasn't driven by ego; it was all a matter of "tea" changing hands before he allowed you in. The tea came in the form of between five and ten shillings. If I had confronted him with the accusation, "You are a bribe-taker," he would have felt terribly insulted. If I had accused him of taking "some tea", he would have taken the accusation more lightly.

That is so because in Kenya, nobody takes bribes; they take tea or "something small", irrespective of the amount of money that has changed hands before a service is given.

The messenger did not take much tea but he made much effort to get it. A person would arrive at the office to apply for a licence to own and carry a sword sheathed to look like a walking stick. The fellow would look at the visitor as if to tell him that entering my office to make that application was a crime. Then he would tell him how difficult it was to see the boss as he was not only in a vile mood but was also opposed to citizens carrying lethal weapons in the open in a peaceful country. He would quote cases of such applications for sword permits that had been denied with a warning, to the applicant never to imagine that he could be allowed to carry weapons.

Having thus terrified the applicant with the consequences of entering my office to apply for a permit, the messenger would tell him, "Perhaps I can try to see the boss on your behalf. It is difficult but I can try." If the applicant did not take the cue and immediately produce some tea or promise some, the messenger would enter my office and walk out with a file which had been awaiting his collection.

21

He would go back to his desk and tell the visitor that he had nearly lost his job a while ago for attempting to speak to me on behalf of a man who wanted a licence to carry a weapon.

However, if the visitor produced the tea, the messenger would pull out a sword permit application form from his drawer, fill it out for the applicant and bring it to me for signature. I would have signed that kind of form with my eyes closed as I considered it a time-wasting formality inherited from the colonial days when an African could not be expected to carry a weapon and not hurt anybody with it.

The case of missing tea has been the cause of many missing files in government offices. The magic of tea has been the cause of the appearance of many missing files.

You wouldn't know the magic of tea before you have gone to a government office having travelled a hundred kilometres from your station of work. You have gone to the head office because for some reason your house allowance has not been credited to your bank for three months.

You report your case to the specific officer who is supposed to handle your case. He listens to you in what looks like a really concerned manner. He then calls for your file from the registry. "Sorry, we cannot find it," the registry says.

It is reported that there is no record of your personal file being taken by any officer yet it cannot be traced inside the registry. You all know that no civil servant takes files home to work on and that files are not Unidentified Flying Objects. The officer all the same looks at you in a way to say that he is as baffled as you are by the case of the disappearing file and that there is nothing that he can do to help you as you are both helpless.

You decide that a file cannot just vanish without explanation from the registry so you go there to do a spot check. You state your case and a clerk points at stacks and stacks of files arranged from floor to ceiling and asks you to make your pick from the lot. You first think that he is joking then you realise he is serious when he goes back to the simple crossword puzzle which he has been working on. You can see that he is more concerned with cracking the clue that says, "The air of melody in an opera", than with the case of a missing file.

You give the stack of files another look and you conclude that you would rather do without your house allowance than attempt to look for your file among the lot. You walk out leaving your case to God. God works in mysterious and devious ways, so as soon as you get into the corridor, somebody says, "Did you find your file brother. Perhaps I can help."

You look at this miracle worker who is offering to find a file that has been declared lost and wonder how he hopes to execute the feat. You are still lost for words when he tells you, "Provided there is something small for the boss."

You want that house allowance which cannot be reinstated before your file has been found, so you give "something for the boss". "And for me?" asks the miracle-worker. They say that when you choose to eat a toad you should pick a fat and juicy one. So now that you have given something for the boss, you also give something to your benefactor. You are told to return in twenty minutes and see the man in the same registry where your file disappeared.

As soon as you part company with your benefactor, he is all smiles because he is the boss who received something in the first instance as well as the file finder. So charged with a double helping of tea, he finds your file which was all long in its place where any of the workers there would have found it.

Once again you appear before the officer who is supposed to solve your case. He studies your file as if it is a fossil in a laboratory. Finally he tells you that your problem cannot be solved on that day and you have to wait for communication at your station of work. You remember that you have come to the head office because you had been writing letters enquiring about your house allowance without any response, so this business of waiting for communication while at your station sounds unconvincing.

You have seen one miracle happen so you initiate the second one by suggesting that since the officer has a stomach you can afford to fill it over lunch. Suddenly you see another miracle happen. The officer says that although it is difficult for your problem to be solved, he can do something about it. He suggests that you see him in the afternoon. Having parted with something small you return at the appointed hour.

Small things move big things because when you return, you have no need for your file. You now need to follow your payment voucher which is lying on the desk of the clerk who is supposed to type it. You now understand that his fingers need inspiration so you energise them with something small. You also energise those of the other clerk who is supposed to pass the voucher as genuine and by the time it gets to the accountant's office, it has been heralded by some tea for boss that you had given to the clerk who was typing the voucher to pass on to his boss.

By the time all the required signatures have been put on the voucher, the cash office is about to close but you need not worry if you have sent something to the cashier to make sure that his window stays open until you get there. Such tea miracles do happen.

Line up and be counted

After ten minutes when I realise that the queue is not moving as fast as it should, I ask why we are there.

The only time I join a queue because indeed there is one, is when there is a shortage of a commodity. Then Kenyans, a people violently opposed to queues for one reason or other, form them behind doors of shops where the scarce commodity is available.

What happens normally is that I am going about other business rather than looking for the missing commodity although the constant grumbling in my house that sugarless tea is the wrong thing in the morning is a constant reminder that I must look for sugar by the end of the day. Then out of the blue, providence seems to provide the missing commodity when I see a queue outside a shop. I automatically assume that the people are queueing for sugar. I join the queue immediately and others line up behind me.

After ten minutes when I realise that the queue is not moving as fast as it should, I ask why we are there. The person ahead of me says, "For maize flour and they won't sell it to you unless you also buy tea leaves." I sneak from the queue because I need sugar and not maize flour.

25

Perhaps such an orderly queue will one day form behind bank counters when there will be a shortage of money. As for now, queues are formed in such places only to be broken. There seems to be such great virtue in jumping queues that the more impunity with which you jump them, the more heroic you are. In the process of jumping the queue, you destroy it and those who were first come last.

A queue-jumper does it in such a civilised way at times that it seems in order to excuse him or her. He finds five or so of you in an orderly queue and, passing the whole lot of you, says, "I have a patient in hospital and I have to get there before the end of visiting hours." He then presents his cheque at the counter before you have responded. His is a way of saying, "Look folks, I am jumping the queue whether you like it or not."

As soon as he is served, somebody else walks in smiling at the teller and after enquiring after each other's health, the visitor presents her cheque and is served before you. That prompts the person at the end of the queue to walk forward and say, "I left my car packed on the yellow line. It might be towed away if I don't get there now." He then presents the bundle of money that he has come to deposit.

You see the futility of queueing and you will instantly bunch around the counter. You simultaneously thrust your cheques and cash deposits on the counter and expect the teller to create some order in the chaos that you have created.

You scrimmage around the counter, none of you willing to step back to allow for easy breathing or access to the teller by anybody else behind you. Should you want to sign up for your money, you have to do an arm tackle to dislodge your hand from somebody else's armpit. After you have received your money, you have to do more arm and foot tackling to get out of the scrimmage.

You head for the *matatu* and bus station where a queue has been formed by the waiting passengers. You join it but as soon as the bus appears at the corner, you find yourself sprinting towards its door before it has stopped. You will sprint because those ahead of you will find no more use in a queue now that the bus has come and will lead you in the race towards its entrance.

Once inside the bus, you will wonder why you nearly broke your leg trying to be the first inside as it will be half empty.

The only time consistent queues were formed in Kenya was when the queue-voting system was in operation. Lining up to be counted behind a candidate of one's choice turned out to be more inviting than making a similar queue at the bus stop after the voting exercise. The queue-voting systems had to go because it turned out that the longest queue was not always the longest in the eyes of the election officials. The shortest one ended up being declared the longest; which went a long way to show that Kenyans can never make good queues.

Toa mashiti

"I spent the night in a fifty," would say a friend known for spending nights out of his house for reasons that don't merit mention here. "Fifty" was his word for a room in an establishment which, like many others in towns, claim to be "boarding, lodging, bar and restaurant" and cost anything from fifty shillings to whatever the proprietor thinks befits the price of a bed.

Such boarding facilities are available in most places in Kenya and range from roadside shacks where they offer breakfast which is invariably a cup of tea, eggs, done at the discretion of the cook who most likely will make them hard fried, and a "toast" which is the name for that buttered slice of bread. The choice is so varied that you can choose to share the bed with bedbugs or spend the night listening to the snoring of a roommate if you are sharing. But you don't need too much effort and money to sleep comfortably.

The imaginative lodging houses call their places motels, inns and taverns, names borrowed from films, books, and magazines without translating the facilities that are found in such places elsewhere into the Kenyan rooms for hire. A Kenyan inn or tavern is generous and offers a bed, a meal, beer and much more.

In North Eastern Province taverns are somewhat thin in those offerings as they follow a Muslim tradition. In Wajir and Mandera, you ask for a bed and not a room. You share a room with a member of your sex and "no sex please because we are Muslims", so your wife or girlfriend shares a room with another woman.

Even with that kind of puritanism, you naturally don't feel too comfortable sharing the room with a stranger. Your mind tells you that the stranger might be a thief who has just come from jail and won't mind going back there for what he considers to be a good catch. So don't feel too guilty if by instinct you take certain precautions such as sleeping in your clothes and having your travelling bag and shoes serve as a pillow.

Elsewhere, the journey to a night in a boarding and lodging, tavern, inn, or whatever, starts at that barred window behind which sits the receptionist.

"A single or double?" he or she asks. A single means a single bed and a double, two beds – sometimes squeezed in a room that is supposed to take one. You take your choice but that inevitably leads to a corridor with rooms facing each other. If you have booked a "self-contained room", there will be a toilet which also serves as a shower room.

If it is not "self-contained", the common toilet and bathroom is at the end of the corridor. There are rubber slippers in the room but if you had designs of walking off with them the following day, you will be disappointed. The pair is either for one foot, meaning they are inconvenient for walking long distances and also embarrassing for wearing in public, or the front is sliced off.

You are weary and have retired to that room for the night and all is quiet. You congratulate yourself on the choice of the room.

The peace and well being last about two hours, then you are awoken by a conversation in the corridor. At first the volume of conversation is controlled and you assure yourself that it will soon end. However, you start hearing each and every word that is being said as if the speakers want you to be a silent participant. The speakers are a male and a female and you can sense that their conversation is oiled by alcohol.

Male: Come on, why are we wasting time. Let us go into the room.

Female: No, I won't go in.

Male: Why now? I thought there was no problem. I thought we had already agreed on the matter.

Female: No we had not agreed on everything.

Male: What kind of person are you? I thought you were mature enough to know that you are not my sister and that...

Female: I also thought you were man enough to know that I have a mouth that does not live on the beer that you have bought. I thought you knew I had a mouth that eats and that I have children who have stomachs.

Male: Those matters can be discussed tomorrow.

Female: No! Tomorrow never comes. They must be discussed now!

Male: Tomorrow, my dear.

Female: Don't dear me. It has to be now.

Male: Tomorrow, I beg you. Why are we...

Female: You are wasting my time.

Male: What about the beer I bought you?

Female: I did not ask for it.

Male: But you drank the beer and ate the chicken. A whole quarter chicken! It cost me fifty shillings.

Female: So what?

Male: Whom are you talking to like that. I spend money on you and then you bring nonsense outside my room. You use the same mouth that has been chewing up my money to insult me? You will see me.

There is brief but very pregnant silence that to you signals peace. Then a male voice booms: "I am not a child and I will prove that to you."

Then follows a succession of thuds, slaps and screams. If the bargaining earlier on had not woken you up, the combat will. You think that it is savage for a man to rain blows on a woman whose only crime is to eat chicken and drink beer bought by a man. So you rise from your bed and with a towel around your waist, you go into the corridor to help the woman.

The man changes the target of his blows from the woman to you amid shouts: "So this woman is your friend, eh? Then why did you not buy her that chicken and beer that I bought? So now you want to take her. You want to steal her from me, eh?"

As you disengage yourself from that battle, you question your wisdom in trying to help the woman as other occupants of rooms on the same corridor stand at their doors, towels around their waists, saying and doing nothing but watching the scene with considerable amusement.

A few hours later, there is loud banging on your door and this time you half-open your eyes and swear not to be engaged in another life-saving mission. The second knock is even louder and you imagine that the irate Romeo has come to take his revenge.

You are proven wrong when with the third knocking, a female voice says, "Toa mashiti!" It is a reminder that it is daylight and that you should hand over the bed sheets if you wish to sleep on. You ignore that order at the risk of the door being banged some more, accompanied by another "Toa mashiti".

Your night in a boarding house need not be a bed of roses. It could be if you book yourself a room where the stairway is smudged and badly lit. A good test for the worth of a boarding house is to ask whether they have rooms for "short term". If the answer is yes, look elsewhere for in such a place there is more than meets the eye.

A piece of leather

I have always considered a game of football a rather silly thing. To me, it is a silly game because I cannot understand how 22 men can spend 90 minutes on pitch sweating it out all in the pursuit of an inflated piece of leather.

That opinion does not make me very popular and I am considered a heretic when I say as much in newspaper columns because to some Kenyans, football is religion.

That is why there is a distinction between football fans and fanatics. Fans maintain some sobriety when their teams lose or win while fanatics become drunk with joy when their teams win and with anger when they lose.

A fanatic defines football thus: "Football is my religion and the pitch is my church. When my team wins, I am filled with the Holy Spirit. When it loses, the Devil enters into me."

The Holy Spirit and the Devil enter many a fanatic as many a time as there are crucial matches. Such a crucial match is inevitably when Gor Mahia and AFC Leopards are playing. The fans and fanatics of each of these teams are identifiable by their attire, the kind of noise they make before, during, and after the match; and even by tribe.

A Gor Mahia fan or fanatic will most likely be a Luo and on the day of a crucial Gor Mahia match will don a sombrero. His rooting chant is *"Gor biro...,"* (Gor is coming) thundered as a final threat to those who doubt the power of the team.

That kind of noise is countered by the throbbing of the Luhya "Isukuti" drums beaten by AFC fans who are predominantly Luhya. The stage is then set for an encounter between teams that draw fans and fanatics from neighbouring regions in Kenya.

Given that the devil and the Holy Ghost can drive fanatics to extremes of meanness and generosity, it is important to know your company well when discussing football, for what you say could be held against you with dire consequences. If you are a practical person who does not like to invite injuries and you are in the company of AFC Leopards fans or, even worse, fanatics, agree with them vigorously on the might of their team. Keep on citing the heroics of the club and particularly its past glory when it was the East and Central Africa Club champion.

Talk ill of Gor Mahia. Call the team's fans hooligans. Agree with the present company that Gor does not stand a chance in the national league against AFC Leopards although the score card says that the opposite situation prevails.

If a while later you find yourself in Gor Mahia company, change your tune. Say that no team in Africa can match the skills of Gor Mahia. Don't call the team just plain Gor Mahia; refer to it as the Mighty Gor. Recall its glory when it won the Nelson Mandela Cup but say nothing about its dismal efforts to regain the title. Call AFC fans, "those good-for-nothing chicken-eaters".

That, of course, means that you cannot claim neutrality in a football match when the two teams are playing by cheering good play and booing a bad game on the part of both teams. Personal safety in the stadium when the two teams are playing is ensured by declaring your loyalty and sitting where other fans of your team are. Only then can you root for your team without inviting a broken skull.

As a fan, you are not in the stadium just to watch a game and root for your team. You also have the added duty of criticising the referee and his linesmen for every real and imagined sin of commission or omission. You become such an expert in soccer rules that you think that you should be officiating instead of the referee and his linesmen.

Should your team lose, that to you has nothing to do with the quality of the team, even if it played like a bunch of kindergarten kids. Blame the referee and as usual mete out instant punishment by rushing onto the pitch to punch him. Then start throwing stones at anything in sight, particularly if it is mobile. Motorists render themselves good targets and you will be doing your duty as a fan to stone as many as possible.

Meanwhile, now that you are in a frenzy and uprooting any shrub that stands in your way as well as shouting the name of your team, don't forget that fans of the other team too are sharp-shooters off the pitch. Watch out for stones that are aimed at you for rooting for your team outside the stadium. If you are wise in this kind of situation, grab one of those plastic seats at the stadium and after banging it on the ground in anger, use it later as a shield against stones thrown by fans of the other team.

If you are like me and you think football is a silly game, it does not mean that you will be safe when there is a crucial match in which, of course, somebody must win and another lose.

Should you, on a Saturday or Sunday afternoon hear the strains of such chanting as "AFC! AFC! AFC!" or "GOR BIRO! GOR BIRO!" change your direction, for you could be on the path of a victory or war march, and in each case it could result in trouble for you .

Even if it is a victory march, there could be trouble for you if you show the kind of disinterest that those who think that football is "chasing an inflated piece of leather for 90 minutes" are likely to exhibit. Your refusal to uproot branches and wave them in celebration could be construed as support for the rival team and an invitation for stones to rain on you.

When the Holy Spirit has seized a football fan following victory on the pitch, he undergoes a complete metamorphosis. The case of what happened to a University of Nairobi anthropology professor tells of the kick that kind of spirit gives to a fan.

The professor was well known for carrying himself about in the lecture halls and on the campus as a fossil. He would deliver his lectures as if he was announcing that the sky would fall in the next minute. But come Saturday when his football team was playing and the man would slip into his weekend wear, and into another personality.

He could be seen among the "Isukuti" drummers dancing to their throbbing drums and chanting praises to his team. When the team lost, he would be seen among the most vigorous stone throwers, capable of rivaling his students who were known for throwing such missiles at the police.

When his team won, the Holy Spirit would inspire him so much that he would be seen dancing in the streets with the other fans without a shirt on. Later he would be seen drinking with abandon at his football club's popular hangout. Only after he ran out of energy (he must have a lot at his age to do all that he did) and wanted to go home would he remember that he had forgotten his car near the stadium, many kilometres away from the final point of the victory celebration.

The truth and nothing but the truth

Once upon a time, people swore by the newspaper: "It must be true. It was in the newspapers."

Now they swear by the accuracy of their ears. "It must be true because I have heard it from a reliable mouth. I have heard it said with my own ears."

Power has gone to the rumour mills and who dares not take them seriously when they sometimes accurately splash the news a day or two before the newspapers? When that happens, more power goes to the rumour mills as elated rumour pedlars say, "Didn't I tell you about this a week ago?"

Other times, something big comes up in the newspapers and if the rumour millers have not been speaking about it, they still don't seem to be in the dark. They will say, "I heard about this thing two days ago", even if they are getting the news for the first time.

A typical big rumour starts from a known event or lack of information about something or somebody who should be in the news.

The mill is kicked into life by somebody saying, "I have not seen the minister for nursery education on television for over two weeks. What do you think is happening?" "Come to think of it. He has not even been in the newspapers for quite some time. It is not like him to be missed out in the news for so long."

The second speaker meets a third one. "What is this I am hearing about the minister for nursery schools? Have you heard it?" "Precisely what I am asking! Don't you think that it is unusual for him to be out of the news? A man's face does not vanish from television screens just like that."

Third speaker to a fourth one: "I am hearing strange things about the minister for nursery schools. Have you heard it? Don't say that I said it but I hear that he has vanished."

Fourth speaker to a fifth one: "I don't know what this country of ours is coming to. How can a whole minister just vanish through the borders like that. There must be something very wrong."

Fifth rumour cog to a sixth Kenyan: "I knew it all the time. I knew that the minister for nursery schools had something up his sleeve. I was right and I am not surprised that he has escaped to the neighbouring country with so much money."

Sixth Kenyan to a seventh one: "Don't say that I said it but I have heard from a reliable source in the Ministry of Nursery Schools that the minister for nursery education is no more. He was killed in the neighbouring country by bandits while escaping with bags of money."

Seventh Kenyan to group of keen listeners: "It must be so because I heard it from my cousin who heard it from his brother who works in the ministry of nursery education. The Minister for Nursery Education is in a critical situation in a hospital in the neighbouring country where he is dying of some unknown disease."

"Could it be Aids?"

"I would not be surprised. The man is known for his liking for young girls."

"No wonder there are so many young girls working in his ministry."

"I know a girl from that ministry who died of Aids."

"I know a guy who had a girlfriend from that ministry. He is also dying of the same disease."

" . . . did you look at that picture of the minister closely?"

"Who would have thought that the disease would reach the minister and his wife?"

"You mean even his wife is dying?"

"What do you expect when her husband is dying."

The next day the minister returns from a quiet overseas trip and members of the press are at the airport to meet him because the rumour that he is dying have reached them. The story has already run in the newsrooms' rumour mills and some of the journalists at the airport are there to test the truth of the rumours. To the chagrin of some of them, the minister is as healthy as ever.

The next day, the newspapers publish a picture of the minister at the airport and instead of that killing the rumours about him, it might put more fire into them.

"Did you look at that picture of the minister closely? Didn't you see a certain uneasiness about him. Didn't you notice that his face was not the usual radiant one?" says a rumour miller.

"He was not even featured on television and when such an event is not covered by the government station it means that the man is out of favour from where it matters."

"I hear that he was not driven in his official vehicle from the airport. He was whisked away by a strange car."

"Was it a blue or red car?"

"A blue one!"

"Then the man is finished!"

"Completely finished."

Meanwhile, the minister is at his house keenly listening to the rumours about his cabinet colleagues for he must catch up with the working of rumour mills.

Street diagnosis

It is very easy to attract a crowd around yourself in the streets of Nairobi because there are those who just love to join in where more than two people are gathered for lack of something better to do. There are also those who join in for profit as a crowd is always good ground for harvesting wallets and purses from those who have gathered there for lack of something better to do.

The easiest way to attract a crowd is just to stop in the street and gaze at nothing in the sky or the top of a building. No sooner have you done that than somebody else will also stop and look up in the direction you are gazing. The two of you will soon be joined by a third, fourth and fifth person all looking intently at nothing in the sky. Having started it all by looking at nothing in the sky, you can sneak away without anybody noticing your absence.

If you return after going around the corner, the crowd will have grown and experts will be giving their opinion on the strange sighting.

"It was there a while ago, I can swear," says one of the people gazing at the sky. "It looked like a flaming ball. I saw it with my own two eyes."

"No, it wasn't like that. You must be blind if you saw something shaped like a ball. It was shaped rather like...you know...like, like..."

"Like a dagger," another Kenyan cuts the speaker short.

"Yes, like a long, thin dagger," says another star gazer.

"There was nothing in the first place," you say with a laugh because you started it all. Suddenly there are many angry stares directed at you and all the eyes that were looking up look at you.

"What is wrong with this fellow?" somebody asks, obviously angry.

"Are you blind or something? I was there and we saw it. Only I don't agree with this man's claim that it was a flaming ball. It was something like...you know...like..."

It is wise to move away at that moment or else you will be engaged in an almost violent argument on the sighting of unidentified flying objects that never were.

You can attract an even bigger and more enthusiastic crowd by fainting in the streets. Not everybody will stop when you faint and some people will actually walk away very fast for fear that you might die and they will be asked to write statements at the police station. These people are insignificant compared to those who will gather around you. The crowd will be so big and so enthusiastic about your fainting that although you need a lot of fresh air, you will get very little of it. You will instead get a lot of hot air from the mouths and bodies of those gathered around you as you lie prostrate on the pavement.

"What happened to him?" somebody will ask to start a conversation.

"How do I know? I was not here when he collapsed," will come the answer because the speaker does not want to be associated with your fainting.

"Is he dead or alive?"

"Looks alive to me but he could be dead. I cannot quite tell because I have never seen a dead man in the streets before." "How could a healthy-looking man just drop down in the street like that?"

"He could have been hit by a falling object. You know such cases have happened before."

"Can't somebody call a taxi to take him to hospital?"

"It looks like a case of malnutrition."

"It could be drunkenness. A case of too much *chang'aa* on an empty stomach."

40

"His breathing looks slow. It looks as if he is going to die."

"Can't somebody call for a taxi to take him to hospital?"

"Who will pay the fare?" "We don't even know the man. He looks about 35 and not very rich. He could be just a civil servant."

Your case will be diagnosed to a terminal stage without anybody giving you as much as the kiss of life as you head for the after-life.

However, there is somebody who would like to do something about you but the crowd is keeping him at bay. The man is a pickpocket who has already mentally diagnosed what you are worth in the pocket. Had the man found you in that state without witnesses, he would have done the most sensible thing to him – clean out your pockets.

Death by remote control

There are times when people don't die from traffic accidents although they were actually crushed into a pulpy mess by a truck in broad daylight. There are times when people don't die of cardiac arrest although the heart specialists say so. They are killed through remote control by an evil eye.

That evil eye is activated by a neighbour who is jealous about that stone house that you have built or by your workmate who is unhappy that you have been promoted before. It might even be said that the remote control death was activated by your wife because she wants to inherit your wealth.

"Not so loud. Is she not a friend of Mary, whose husband died last year?"

As you lie in the coffin with the Catholic priest sprinkling your remains with holy water, a conversation is going on at the back of the church. "How could the car just get off the road when it had no puncture or anything like that?"

"Impossible! That car could not have behaved like that and killed our friend who now lies dead. Things don't go that way."

"How many people have met such accidents and yet they have not even been scratched? Many of course!"

"I hate to say this but I think that car was sent to finish him. That is why it just got off the road and killed our friend."

"I thought so myself. And for that to happen when he had just taken a loan to start a shop. How unfair can life be?"

"It is not life; it is his enemies. I always told him to beware of his enemies and be modest about his achievements but he would not listen."

"This world does not like people doing well. That car must have been sent to finish him off by his enemies. I wonder who it could be."

"These days you cannot trust anybody. It is unwise to even trust your wife although she shares the same bed with you."

"I agree with you entirely. Wives have become very dangerous. Who knows, this wife of our friend, has she..."

"Not so loud. Is she not a friend of Mary, whose husband died last year? Is it not said that whoever keeps the company of a thief also becomes a thief? We know Mary's husband died in car accident and now our friend has died in similar circumstances. I don't want to say it but isn't it too much of a coincidence?"

"I thought so as well and now that you mention Mary, one can see the possibilities. Our friend did not just die. The car was sent by somebody close to him, most likely his wife."

"Wait a minute! Do you see what I am seeing? The wife of our late friend has fainted. It must be out of shock and sorrow."

"I doubt that. It must be the excesses of what she did to her husband that have gotten into her."

Those who do such unconscious public relations for the power of the evil eye say the power of those who control it is such that all you need to do is pay a consultation fee to them and all is done. It is said that all you need to do after paying that fee is to name your target and the rest will follow. The target will choke on a bone, step on a banana peel and break his cranium or simply drop dead.

If the kind of man I visited when I was doing a story on astrologers and exhumers of evil eyes is the type that works remote control deaths, then I must have chosen the wrong one.

I chose an "astrologer" who had been advertising himself in the newspapers as having a cure-all for such problems as unemployment, unsteady love affairs, fears of the evil eye directed by an enemy and a myriad of other problems.

43

He was none of the mumbo jumbo-chanting witchdoctors of comics and films wearing a colobus monkey cap, but a suave urbane man operating from a relatively comfortable hotel room. My problems were not really astounding and included having a girlfriend who was dominating my life although I was married and that I tended to spend money as soon as I earned it.

After that he took my palm, traced the main lines on it with a pen and scribbled yet something else on the index.

The first problem did not exist but the second one was real as it had affected other Kenyans who were living in inflationary times.

He asked me the name of my girlfriend and after scribbling something in Arabic on an index card, he took two vials which were

44

on a table. He then spread out a piece of newspaper. He poured a powder that looked like sawdust from one vial onto the newspaper. He poured some drops of oil from the other vial and chanted something unintelligible. Then right in front of my eyes sprung a fire that consumed the piece of newspaper. Moses could not have been more surprised when he saw a burning bush on Mount Sinai without anything obvious causing it.

The man's very clear eyes looked into mine and I was sure he was trying to read something in them. After recovering from the surprise of the sudden flame, I was sure he was checking my eyes to see how much his trick of surprise and attack had worked.

After that, he took my palms, traced the main lines on it with a pen and scribbled something else on the index card.

Having diagnosed the cause of my problems through fire and palmistry, he gave the cause of my suffering.

He told me, with the self assurance of a medical practitioner who had just looked at laboratory tests results or an ulcer: "That girl friend of yours intends to finish you off by taking charms that are worse than somebody digging a grave for you. She has snared you so much through those spirits that you need help before all is gone. It will cost you eight hundred shillings."

I had taken imprest to cover such high expenses and as soon as I had paid the man, he reached for a jar of a cure. He scooped some brown paste from it, something like cocoa paste and put it into a vial.

"Take a teaspoonful of this medicine when you wake up in the morning and before you go to bed." Then he produced a piece of bark from another jar and told me to chew it. I asked him when and he said I could do that at that moment. I had a mind to dash to the door and make good my escape but another voice in my head told me that the man was capable of "arresting" me with his medicine if I tried to do so.

I chewed the piece of bark and it did not taste like anything I can remember. As I chewed the bark, he gave me a sewed up piece of leather the size of a thumb nail.

"Carry this in your wallet all the time. It will protect your money."

I opened up the piece of leather later in the office and inside it was some white powder wrapped in a newspaper. To this day, I still spend money as fast as I make it. I blame inflation, not my failure to keep the piece of charm inside my wallet.

Rost and mboilo

There used to be no doubt why a Maasai warrior could strangle a male lion bare-handed. It was all in the stomach, so seemed to suggest ethnologists. The ethnologists energetically said the Maasai fed predominantly on meat and blood from their livestock.

The stomachs of the Maasai have apparently now overtaken the observations of ethnologists, some of whom still voraciously paint the Maasai and other nomadic tribes as doing nothing more than dart the jugular vein of an animal or simply floor it when they need a meal. Perhaps they have not seen fierce-looking warriors, one leg on the knee, eating a bun and drinking a Coca Cola. They have been co-opted into the junk-food culture. They have lost the meat-eating culture to other Kenyans who have pounced on the habit with the vociferousness of warriors.

Whoever called Kenya a man-eat-man society some years ago would today be tempted to call it a man-eat-meat society. A national pastime that appetisingly engages the time of middle income earners, the new culture has been blamed for the now popular ailment, gout. Gout, also called the rich man's disease, has caused quite a limp among rich and middle class Kenyans, and once you acquire it, it is assumed that you have been gorging yourself with meat, particularly the roasted type.

Gout or no gout, butchers continue to make a kill from the carnivorous habits of Kenyans over lunch hour, in the evenings, over those long meat eating sessions during weekends and indeed any time.

The butcher operates his shop like a restaurant but only with one item on the menu: meat, of course. Thus, while you can buy your own piece of meat to take home, you can also have it roasted, boiled or fried at his shop, which is normally anywhere you need it.

Every butcher worth his cut advertises his service with a big mural depicting a goat or a cow at the top of his shop. In North Eastern Province, paintings of camels announce the availability of camel meat.

"Kiongo and Sons Butchery Ltd," the sign says, and below that, "Special Rost and Mboilo. Steak, Chaps, Matumbo, etc." All Kiongo is saying is that facilities for roasting and boiling meat are available and so are such cuts as steak, chaps and offals. "Etc" includes such other things as boiled goat heads and legs.

I don't have to go to Kiongo's place to make my order for boiled meat. The telephone does it. "Kiongo," I say on telephone, "Make it three kilos of the best cut from the ribs."

"Beef or Mutton?"

"Beef of course. Don't make it too lean or too fat. Just in between. Make four cups of soup from it. Not too thin not too thick."

"With what?"

"Half a kilo of potatoes, the same quantity of tomatoes and, just wait a minute..."

"I have just eaten a rotten piece of meat!"

I cover the mouthpiece to speak to one of the friends in the office who is coming along with me for lunch, "Hey, do you like little or much green pepper in your meat?" I get an answer and back to Kiongo, "just a little pepper to season it. Don't forget onions and tomatoes. How long?...forty five minutes? Beautiful! We will be there in that time...Yes, I said four cups of soup, the best that you can make from the meat."

Forty five minutes later, I am at Kiongo's with three friends, one of whom has agreed to come along because we have assured him that the meat is boiled. Like many other Kenyans, he is convinced that boiled meat is gout free and roast meat the cause of the national limp.

Kiongo has a modicum of hygiene and we wash our hands with hot water that flows from a cylinder at the door to the butchery. The water is heated with charcoal embers at the bottom of the metal cylinder.

The meat tastes alright for sometime until one of us pauses from finishing the piece that he is chewing. He looks at the rest of us to check whether we are getting the same experience that he is undergoing. On seeing that we are chewing on happily, he all the same comments, "I have just eaten a rotten piece of meat."

None of us is surprised because although Kiongo is generally a reliable man, he is not averse to throwing in a small piece of stale meat to make the weight and hope that it will not be noticed in the midst of the rest which, to say the least, is first class. We clear the tray of meat and drink our soup in a way of saying that we really don't mind Kiongo behaving like his fellow butchers who throw a piece of bone or a not-so-fresh piece of meat on the scale to make the required weight.

We share the cost of the meat which includes such items as "fire", which is Kiongo's word for boiling or roasting charges.

Gout or no gout, we are sure that we have just had one of the cheapest yet most filling meals in the city as we walk back to the office.

A necklace for all sizes

Had Pontius Pilate been a governor in Kenya and presided over the trial of Jesus Christ in Nairobi, he would have attracted a crowd quite enthusiastic to pass judgement on the accused.

Not a crowd really, but a mob ready to dispense "mob justice." By a quirk of linguistic manipulation "mob justice" has come to mean instant dispensation of violence on a suspect judged by a motley crowd in the street for one of the various crimes so punishable.

The street penal code judges and passes sentence on such crimes as pick-pocketing, theft from motor vehicles, purse-snatching, necklace-snatching. In other words it caters mainly for petty street crimes.

The penal code can be expanded though to cover such crimes as the chairman of The Hawkers Association selling out to the city authorities, a member of one tribe attacking another for what may be tribal or non-tribal reasons, or a "spy" being spotted in an interest group.

Street "justice" is triggered by the word "Thief", perhaps yelled by a woman who is hugging her own bosom to indicate where her stolen purse was. Don't protest your innocence if you are standing next to her. That could be construed as admission of guilt.

You could be out of luck though if that woman's instincts tell her that since you are the person closest to her, then it follows that your hand dipped into her bosom and stole her purse. In that case you could take one of the two options open to you.

You could plead innocence and show your empty pockets to prove it – but that won't absolve you from culpability and the subsequent punishment, or you could choose the option of wrenching yourself from the grip of the woman and making a run for it, which will prove to the now gathered mob that you are guilty. This option is open if you are either an Olympic sprinter and stunt man or an accomplished street thug, or if a policeman is in sight. The presence of a policeman benefits both the guilty and innocent suspect who, to escape "mob justice", must hug the policeman in a desperate embrace.

It is even safer to take refuge in a police car if there is one in sight, for then the hands of "justice" will be a safe distance from you.

Let's assume that, whether guilty or innocent, you decide to sprint to safety and there is no policeman or police car in sight. There are several possibilities:

You could be run over by a car while running across the road, if you are not that accomplished thief capable of dodging drivers who want to kill you, not because you are a suspected thief, but because they are fond of killing anyway.

You could also find an escape route without murderous drivers and actually find that your feet are quite agile for your age and that your chest can take the punishment of a pounding heart and overstretched lungs. That is not surprising considering that you can hear behind you, a stampede caused by your pursuers.

The noise naturally alerts those in the direction where you are heading and they, too, don't need much to be fired into a mood to dispense "justice". So behind and ahead of you are people armed with "tools" of "justice".

In what might be called the stone age era, Kenyan mobs used stones to dispense street "justice". Then came the nineties and they went into the rubber age and their tools of "justice" became old tyres to fit all sizes.

Tyre "justice" was an import from South Africa where the crime of being a political traitor was punished by the necklacing of the victim with a tyre and setting it aflame.

So if Pontius Pilate sat over the judgement of Jesus Christ in Kenya and asked the mob what to do with Jesus, they would reply, "Necklace him! Necklace him!" Jesus, however, would not have to carry his own tyre. They would carry it for him to the pyre.

One of the most memorable pictures carried in the Kenyan press was that of a man, judged guilty and sentenced to burn "till dead" by necklacing, being led to his Calvary.

He was the chairman of the Nairobi City Hawkers Association and his crime was the betrayal of his members. No less punishment was thought fit for such a traitor.

He was pictured being held by the seat of his trousers and the scruff of his neck by one man flanked by a crowd while another man rolled a tyre along. It seemed too casual even for a nightmare but the lot meant business. The appearance of armed police ruined the show.

Had anybody else tried to ruin the show, there was a chance that the mob would have turned on him and accused him of being an accomplice in the crime that the man was supposed to have committed. An accomplice gets equal punishment with the first accused.

If you don't wish to cast the first stone, then don't cast the first word in defence of a "mob justice" suspect.

Guilty, your honour

There is a chance of ending up in police custody and eventually before a magistrate. There are many reasons why you could be arrested.

Lack of proper identification papers renders you open to such criminalised labels as "illegal immigrant", "vagrant", "loiterer with intent", "prostitute" and others!

Walking in town at night with what the police impute to be little money could be another since your relative poverty could be interpreted to mean that you have a propensity for stealing.

If you are a lady of virtue and going about your business in the streets in the dark, you might qualify for the cells and for an appearance before a magistrate. The police will consider it their duty as custodians of the law and morality to keep you away from the public in these days of Aids.

You might end up in the cells for drinking in an unlicensed night club which you found open and whose license you did not demand to see since you didn't consider it your business. There is a chance of also being arrested for drinking before or after hours.

Let's say the police have told you that they are arresting you for failing to have proper identification papers and since it is night, bail is not available. You spend the night in the cells and the following day you are transported to court.

You have decided to plead guilty since it is a fact that you did not have those papers. The best you hope for is to mitigate for a lenient sentence, pleading that you indeed have your papers but you forgot them at home.

The final moment comes in the court cells when the police prosecutor starts calling out names of suspects who are due to appear before the magistrate. Your name is called along with those of other suspects and you all file into the court.

As ten or so of you are directed to the dock, you begin to expect the worst. You tell yourself that if so many of you are facing the same charge, that is lacking proper identification papers, then the court is likely to take a dim view of you.

You can already imagine the court prosecutor pleading with the court to give a "custodial sentence" saying that the big number of suspects facing the same charge is an indication that the said crime has become so prevalent that it must be stopped forthwith.

52

Then the magistrate calls out the name of one of the people in the dock and reads out the charge.

"You were arrested at 3 a.m. in the streets of Nairobi drunk and disorderly."

"Guilty, your honour."

"Three hundred shillings fine or three months in prison in default."

The next suspect is called, the same charge read and similar guilt admitted. A similar sentence is imposed.

The same goes for the third and fourth suspect and then it is your turn. You have gone over the words of your mitigation several times and you are ready to roll them out.

You rub your ear lobes to find out whether you still have ears when the charge is read. You find that they are still there and as you do, the magistrate is gazing at you waiting for your plea.

Your charge is being drunk and disorderly at an ungodly hour and you are certain that at the hour of the alleged crime, you were stone sober, lying on the cement floor of your cell.

"Guilty or not guilty?" the magistrate repeats.

"Not guilty."

"I order you to be remanded in custody. Your case will be mentioned in two weeks."

Two weeks is a very long time in custody. At times admission of guilt when charged with a crime different from that which you were arrested is in order. That is if you are not masochistic enough to prefer to go back to the cells and insistent enough to make the arresting officer charge you with the original crime of lacking proper identification papers.

It does not always happen that way but the police seem to have a penchant for substituting certain misdemeanours with the charge of drunk and disorderly. It saves them the time they would spent giving evidence and responding to cross-examination since it is a charge that is almost readily admitted.

It is a charge that is likely to destroy your reputation considerably when mouthed by some court interpreters. When the charge is read as plainly as "you are charged that you were drunk and disorderly", they turn it into, "you were arrested so drunk that you were urinating all over the place".

The prosecutor will later say before you are sentenced, "This kind of crime, your honour, has become prevalent and should be punished with a custodial sentence to act as a deterrent."

The only place you could have wished to empty your bladder at the hour of committing the alleged crime was in your cell where at 3 a.m. in the morning, that call of nature was quite pressing.

However, although you could smell the pail into which you were supposed to relieve yourself, you could not get access to it without walking over somebody.

You obviously don't step on strangers who have been muttering all night that they are going to kill somebody as soon as they are out, unless you wish to be included in their murder list.

Fate has its own ways, and blame it if next morning you are ordered to empty the overflowing pail though you did not use it at all in the night or at any time during your stay in the cells.

That is not worse than being described as "helping the police with investigations", for that might mean that you are somewhere in a police cell and that the police are not baby-sitting you but trying to talk evidence out of you through several methods, including what they call using "reasonable force".

Worse still is the chance of being turned into a newspaper photograph and caption titled, "Most wanted criminal shot dead". The photograph will most likely have you with the gun that you have allegedly shot your way to fame with on your chest. You will have no chance to wonder why all those guns that "most wanted criminals" have look like those that the police use.

Have you heard?

Kenya is a land of "true" rumours and of fertile imaginations. It is also a land where despite the arrival of the satellite, the bush telegraph sometimes works more efficiently than the mass media.

The true rumours many times happen to be what everybody knows to be true but which nobody wants to talk about openly so it must be, "I have heard this but I don't know whether it is true or not." Finally it might be published and then it will be, "I told you, didn't I?"

By the time what started as rumour is published, it will have been refurbished so many times that it will have no resemblance to what has been passed on by the rumour mills.

Kenyans put a distinction between rumours and gossip. Rumours are about serious matters such as politics and public figures while gossip is what women talk about when they are drawing water.

The explosion of a car tyre could churn out one of the biggest rumour stories of the day. Let us say that Nairobi City Council wardens have been engaged in a running battle with hawkers, as they are known to sometimes do, with bloody results.

A lorry tyre bursts somewhere near the City Hall. A man hears the explosion from a distance on his way to take a bus to his rural home. He hurries to the bus as his mind has told him that the explosion cannot be anything but gunfire.

One hour later, he is talking about the explosion at his rural market. "I tell you people," he says, "I don't know what Nairobi has become. When I left there, there was nothing in the air except gun explosions."

An hour later, the story has been picked by another wavelength of the bush telegraph and somebody is telling another, "I have heard that people are dying in Nairobi like houseflies."

The listener passes on the story, "I hear that a hundred people have died in Nairobi today. I have heard it from my neighbour who works there."

Another version surfaces a while later and it is that people are fleeing from the city in their hundreds because of the violence that has erupted there.

By the end of the day, there might be reports on the houses that have been burned down, the vehicles destroyed, and the hundreds of people maimed.

The following day there might be a three line news item in the newspapers reporting on a tyre explosion and the rumour about deaths will die a sudden death.

A matter of life and death

When prominent Kenyans die, they are eulogised that the gap they have left will be very difficult to fill. Of course the gap they have left in their places of employment is filled as fast as the grave, the moment they are down.

Such a Kenyan may have died from a motor accident induced by drunken driving but then it will be said at his grave side that the "cruel hand of fate has grabbed our brother" and his death will be described as "untimely".

Many prominent people are reported of dying "after a short illness" which gives birth to the thought that this short illness is some sort of an undisclosed virus.

At the funeral of a well known thief, it was said, "Our dear departed brother has been called by the Lord because He likes good people to be close to Him in heaven."

The deceased does not always get such a send-off among some communities where the dead must be chastised even if they cannot see or hear.

WHAT BUSINESS DO YOU HAVE COMING TO PRETEND THAT MY DEATH HAS SADDENED YOU....

At one such funeral, an aunt walked over to the coffin carrying her nephew and addressed it as if she was sitting by the fire with the deceased. "I warned you!" she fumed.

"I warned you not to buy a car and instead buy a farm. You refused to listen to me and where are you now? Dead. Can you drive a car now? No! It killed you. You can't say I did not warn you."

A friend from the Luhya community where that is reported to have happened, claims that the dead too can answer back. He claims that when the relatives of a departed man filed past his body to pay their last respects, the dead person was angry about the presence of his brother with whom he had not been getting along.

My informant claims that the dead person opened his eyes and shouted at his brother, "What business do you have coming to pretend that my death has saddened you? Go away! You never had time for me when I was alive."

The same friend claims that that is not the only incident among his people when the dead have defied the saying that "Dead men tell no tales".

If the departed could sigh, they would do so with relief to finally rest in the grave having been transported hundreds of kilometres from the city where the death occurred, for the dead must be buried at their ancestral homes or where the deceased owned land.

Public cemeteries are for those who have cut ties with the rural areas for one of various reasons, including having lost ancestral land or having been so urbanised as to specify in the will that the burial should take place in a public cemetery in the city.

The long journey home is the culmination of funeral wakes sometimes taking place simultaneously in several places. The kind of wake the deceased gets depends on where he or she came from and which religion he or she subscribed to.

One thing is almost certain in all cases and it is that there will be plenty of music. African drums will throb night after night until the last day of the wake if the deceased belonged to one of the independent African churches found all over Kenya.

There will be dance music and even dancing if the deceased was a Luo. Part of the takings from the wake will go to buying batteries to keep the music running.

The Luo people are legendary for turning funeral wakes and the after-the-burial rituals into one big banquet at the expense of the family of the deceased but hard times have popularised the habit.

As a result, professional mourners are to be found everywhere, crying, as Nigerian novelist Chinua Achebe says, more than the relatives of the deceased.

There is profit in a river of crocodile tears and the case of the mourner who found none flowing from his eyes may perhaps say to what lengths some people can go to induce them.

The mourner found that food trays at the funeral wake were avoiding his path and concluded that he needed an incentive to make the servers notice him.

So he went out and fired himself with a good dose of *chang'aa* whose fast-acting effects transformed him instantly. On his return, a short while later, he was a flood of tears and threatening to throw himself into the grave that had been dug for the deceased. The food servers could not ignore him any more.

In the circumstances where the living believe that the relatives have no right to the deceased person's property, a situation that pertains to some communities, the living suddenly find that they shared physical dimensions with the late.

His clothes are scattered across the ridges among those who claim, "the deceased had shoulders as big as mine... He had a waist as slim as mine... He was my uncle or my cousin and we wore the same length of trousers".

As in a marriage ceremony, the bigger the convoy of vehicles leading the deceased to his grave, the bigger the fame. Private cremations and burials are an anti-social habit, a statement that the deceased was not a person of the people.

A funeral that is partly handled by the funeral parlours that are a new event in Kenya enhances the image of the family of the deceased more than that of the deceased and so is the size of the death announcement advertisement in the newspapers.

The announcement at times serves the purpose of advertising the curriculum vitae of the deceased person's relatives.

Its wording might leave no doubt that the late will be missed by people of substance when it reads, "The Late Mr Dead was a cousin to Dr Alive, managing director, Death Industries, Yvonne of Sussex University, uncle to Darius, Company Secretary Parlour Services and Professor Mortis, a Nairobi gynaecologist".

The untitled appear at the end of the advertisement and are cited as "The late Mr Dead was also the brother to Tom, Mark and Harry".

Till dowry do us join

Whenever my father came home inspired by a number of lagers, he would remind us all that in his house was a girl who would one day bring him a thousand shillings in dowry.

A thousand shillings was a lot of money in the early sixties, the equivalent of the number of goats and other livestock that traditionally made up the bride price.

That kind of money today would not be enough even to carry out the investigations that some fathers undertake to find out the money value of their potential sons-in-law.

The value and the commercial attachment that is now pegged on bride price instigates such fathers to do a reconnaissance on the capacity of their potential sons-in-law to pay a handsome dowry.

The family of the eligible bachelor in the end gets what is in effect, a shopping list from his future in-laws. The list might include a water tank or its equivalent in cash to "compensate the mother of the bride for the labour she underwent drawing water from the river to bring up her daughter".

The father might suggest that a "four-wheel barrow" is in order as part of the bride price. Such a contraption is nothing less than a half-ton pick-up which yet another word acrobat could call a "tray to help an old man fend for his cattle".

There might be an item earmarked for the clan for "helping to bring up a daughter worth marriage".

Such transactions would normally involve a sympathetic bank manager who in this case is replaced by friends of the bride who are persuaded through pre-wedding parties to raise the dowry.

A pre-wedding party might not be just a dowry-raising party. It can also be a successful fundraiser to finance the wedding, the couple's "just married" first car or a plot on which to build a house.

You get the idea when you get to the door of the party's venue. A bevy of beauties are normally stationed there like front-line soldiers armed with carnations and pins.

Before you can ask whether you are in the right place, there is a carnation on your lapel, accompanied by disarming smile and a stretched hand. "That will be fifty shillings, sir," you are told in a manner to suggest that "goods once sold cannot be returned."

You get more suggestions that you are in a more than "willing giver, willing taker" situation as the party warms up. You have already joined the queue of the donors and handed over what you intended to contribute and now you are on the dance floor enjoying the music.

The music dies off suddenly and the master of ceremonies announces that a generous donor has stopped the music with a specific sum of money and that whoever wants it to resume is free do so with a donation.

For the next hour, there is a see-saw of music being stopped by a donation only to be restarted with yet another donation until the gimmick wears out. The show is not yet over as the master of ceremonies announces that the bride has sworn that she will refuse to get married if all the bald men in the party don't "persuade" her to do so by standing up and donating generously.

Since you are not bald you think that you are safe, a notion that is dispelled when it is announced that the bridegroom has sworn to remain a bachelor all his life if all the married men in the party don't change his mind by donating so generously that he is convinced that marriage is a good idea.

The wedding day is invariably on a Saturday and more likely at the end of the month when gift purchasing power is potent.

The gifts depend on who is marrying who but a bed for the couple is in order in Central Kenya and since Africans don't blush, the bride and bridegroom are asked to sit on it to gauge its suitability for future use.

In the same region, there is talk of money marrying money — that is the son of a rich man marrying into a rich family. Then the gifts can be a statement of "My Mercedes is Bigger than Yours".

The father of the bride will say, "I have a small gift for this couple" and then unruffle a piece of paper which will turn out to be a deed poll donating a house to the bride and bridegroom.

The mother of the bride, as if not be outdone, will announce that she too has brought "something small" that will ensure that her daughter does not "let her husband go hungry". The "something small" could be a fridge big enough to hold a whole cow.

The parents of the bridegroom might be motivated enough to say that "My daughter-in-law needs a shopping basket to enable her to feed her husband." A shopping basket in this case is a saloon car.

Given that the business of water tanks and "trays for fending for the cattle" as well as motivating friends and well-wishers to donate generously can be a disincentive in marriage matters, there is always the alternative of "come-we-stay".

Some call it trial marriage but as sometimes happens, it stays long enough to be "till death do us part".

In the church marriage it could be "till the rival do us part", and even that happens at that moment when the nine-month pregnant bride who has donned a bridal gown and the face of a virgin is at the altar beside her bridegroom.

Just then enter a court orders server with an order issued by the magistrate stopping the wedding. Apparently the bridegroom has been having a "come-we-stay" affair with another woman and the products are two children.

Such fairy tale weddings that never were are not the stuff of fiction.

A rose by another name

There is a joke that in colonial Kenya, the white man in charge of rat eradication was known as a rodent officer. When the job was Africanised, the holder of the office became a rat catcher.

In those days, a letter addressed to a married woman said specifically that it was meant for "Mrs House Wife, w/o Mr Town Worker". Now it will most likely be addressed to Ms House Wife.

Then, a managing director rode back left in a limousine. Now, he carries a calling card announcing that he is indeed a managing director, but he does not know where his next meal will come from.

Now that calling cards cost a shilling a piece, a carpenter can claim on one that he is the managing director of "Joe Furniture Works", which happens to be the business name of the shed where he operates from.

It is all a statement of how Kenyans like titles and how titles lose and gain value. It also says something about their ineptitude.

A company executive knows that he has been shown the door when he ceases to be the group personnel officer and gains such "promotion" which now changes his title to "Executive Officer in charge of Staff Motivation.

Professor Bahati Mbaya, announced by a business sign board that he can cure lung cancer, Aids and epilepsy, among other ailments through herbs, has never seen the inside of a high school. Neither has Dr Dawa, his fellow herbalist.

For the rural folk, that nurse who runs the clinic deserves no less title than "doctor" and so does the veterinary man whose only preoccupation is providing artificial insemination to livestock.

It is possible to get a letter headed, "From the Desk of Mr Mheshimiwa, Former Minister for Health" lest you forget that he was once what he was.

The person introduced as, "Mr Cash, a banker," is no more than a novice teller in a bank, while a businessman is anybody ranging from a kiosk owner to a gold exporter.

Five years ago, the gas station next to where I lived was renovated and up went a sign reading, "STATION OPEN UNDER NEW MANAGEMENT". The sign still stands, now worse for colour and the same could be said of the management.

The number of businesses bearing the claim "new" suggest that there is some magic in the word, though it at times reflects the work of stretched imagination. "New Modern Green Bar" sees paint only when the health inspectors insist on it, and its potholed floor reminds you of the faces of its customers.

Matatu operators, though, find nothing "new" and original in the word. Instead, they scream that among them are the good, the bad and the ugly.

A matatu christened "Public enemy" shares the road with "Praise the Lord!" The latter will hog the road with "Chicago Bulls" which has just almost made "By Public Demand" go off the road.

A kindergarten, a pre-primary unit or even a junior academy could be anything from a converted bedroom where children are taken to while away the time by doodling on the floor, to an institution where they use the Montessori teaching method. The head of either institution could claim to be a "principal".

Political talk

When the person referred to always as "His Excellency the President" does a public function, the national radio reports him as having addressed a "mammoth crowd". The idea here is not to suggest any prehistoric association between the occasion and that fossilised mammal but to say that never has a bigger event taken place.

The same report will say that the President "warned enemies of development". Here one almost sees a battalion of people, daggers drawn, facing this thing called development. One can almost picture those "enemies of development" waylaying it in a dark alley.

He will be reported as having warned those enemies "amid cheers and thunderous applause". One can see flashes of applause cutting across the sky

A day later, the media will report that a certain Member of Parliament has disassociated himself and his constituents from the activities of those enemies of development and "condemned in the strongest terms" the activities of those people.

He will add, "My loyalty and that of my constitueny to the government is total and direct." Talk about missiles set on a target!

In the daily newspapers, there will be a report about a minister pledging that the "government will leave no stone unturned until the culprits have been brought to book".

The statement is reported so often that one gets the feeling that the Government is made up of masons and printers.

The same minister will promise such punishment to the culprits whom he will have accused of "pouring out money to finish me". You might wonder whether the man is scared of being drowned in a deluge of money.

Despite such threats to his life by a flood of currency notes, the man will promise his audience that the government "will work round the clock to solve your problems". Once again this statement is repeated so often that one gets the impression that the government is a clock watcher.

Any of those politicians reported as having said this and that entered politics in the first instance because they were allegedly answering the "irresistible calls by the people to stand for elections".

The call is so loud and irresistible that the politician has to beg and borrow money so that he can have enough to bribe the voters.

Being an elected leader, he has to be introduced at public meetings before making a speech. It will be said that he is about to "greet his people" and say a "few words". An hour later, he will still be greeting "his people" and saying a "few words".

Among his "few words", he will advise his listeners that "education is the key to the future", as if they are hearing about education for the first time.

He will advise them to "plant early since rains are on the way", as if rains are a strange phenomenon and as if he works for the meteorological department.

He will also most likely advise them to be on the lookout for "enemies of development, hiding in tea bushes, ready to subvert our hard-won independence".

Part of parliamentary language for a cabinet minister is to recite, "The project will be implemented when funds become available", and tell Kenyans to work harder so that the country can get the "much-needed and scarce foreign currency".

"When funds become available" in the circumstances of scarce foreign currency means "such a project can wait till judgement day". Foreign currency is a much sought for commodity but not "foreign masters working in cohort with their local puppets", often accused of being saboteurs "out to create fear and despondency".

Ask the politician to substantiate the claims about such saboteurs and say which train they have derailed and the answer will be, "I don't run my affairs through the press."

The same person will some days later complain that the media have given him a blackout because they have been bought out by "my detractors to finish me".

Born in Kenya, made in America

I was once James Brown Wahomey, though I had never set my foot in the United States or in any other part of the world except where I was born.

However, James Brown and soul music had come to my part of the world via the radio and the gramophone and taken over my life. I announced that my other name was Soul Brother Wahomey by emblazoning the fact with a felt pen on my jacket and by saying "I am black and proud" with a withered American drawl.

There has never been an American called Wahomey but I was hoping that by the grace of God the fact that I had added a consonant to a name from a language group that uses only vowels, I would be americanised.

My legacy is all over the streets of Nairobi in the person of Jane Jack, the girl from Western Kenya. She is Jane all right and her father is Jack. She is also Atieno and her father Onyango but Atieno

Onyango is out for it evokes the village and Jane Jack is in because it suggests that her ancestry is Caucasian, urban and urbane.

She is not like the Maggie Blackie of my age who wore a wig that sat incongruously on her head like a misplaced bird nest. Instead, she prefers what she calls "human hair", a hair piece that is bought in the beauty parlours.

It is wavy and conceals her natural kinky hair, but as for being "human", there is considerable doubt. "Human" is supposed to contrast with "natural" and the former, like the wig, is covering up for the claimed shortcoming of the latter.

Brother Rasta Lefty, born and brought up in central Kenya, also has some legacy from Soul Brother Wahomey. Wahomey used to wear a face that suggested that he was annoyed with the world all the time although he was black and proud.

In those days, it was said that Wahomey's type had to look like a "cool cat". Rasta Lefty takes his face from the Caribbeans and he wears what he calls a stone face.

A creation of reggae music and the rasta culture, he picks his models from the "life-is-a-serious-business" poster pinups of his heroes from that culture.

So he sports pitch black Gandhi spectacles and, of course, dreadlocks. Then he screws his face into a stony mask.

Wahomey tried to speak with a Texan drawl. Rasta Lefty tries to make himself incomprehensible by mouthing Caribbean pidgin mostly picked up from the words of reggae music.

It would seem then that Kenya's popular culture moves to the rhythm of other worlds, a fact that a young man wearing a punk hair cut and an earring should attest to.

Rap and funk course through his blood and so do Coke and hamburgers. Matatu operators who hardly have time for television, if they can afford sets for that matter, keep pace with Magic Johnson and the Los Angeles Lakers. At least they salute them with the gay painting of those names on their vehicles.

I am still black and proud, but not Wahomey any more. Being black and proud, I have some West African costumes which I wear once in a while.

The reactions I get when I am in them are typical of Kenyans' attitudes to suits. The reaction is normally, "You look relaxed today. Are you not working?"

Thus, the suit is supposed to suggest your frame of mind. It is supposed to be a complimentary tool to your brain, an accessory that you carry on you to the office in the blazing January sun because as former Malawian president, Kamuzu Banda, is quoted to have said, "A gentleman is a gentleman in Cairo's summer or in the Cape Town's winter".

Such gentlemen who defy the elements of weather are to be found all over Kenya. They are to be found wrapped in woollen suits in church on Sundays in the humidity and the blazing sun of Mombasa.

They are to be found on court benches simulating winter conditions in the Nairobi January heat, with their three-piece suits which are judicial robes and wigs on their heads.

They wear ill-fitting suits – because that is what they can afford – so that they can step out to visit friends.

Those who can afford expensive ones step out in them on national days, red carnations on their lapels, to watch traditional dances in the stadia among other activities. In their speeches later, they talk about the importance of "preserving African culture" as they finger their silk ties.

During the evening parties on those national days, they spot their tail suits as they watch yet another session of African dances. Their wives throw in a sprinkle of colour with typically West African costumes. Yet another speech is made about the importance of preserving African culture.

Their children have some legacy from Wahomey, too. They like to take particular pride in their inability to speak any Kenyan language.

No warnings please, we are Kenyans

Perhaps even Kenyan weathermen don't take umbrellas with them even when they have predicted rain in a nation where warnings are taken to mean the exact opposite of what they say.

In Kenya, red traffic pedestrian lights mean a licence for the horde of people who have come to that point to cross as if they have been put on automatic gear. They take it as a challenge to force the on-coming traffic which has the right of way to come to a screeching halt accompanied by a chorus of hooting.

It is at times some sort of dare to the same vehicular traffic that confuses zebra crossing for "no pedestrian zone" and tears through red lights with the fury of meteors, scattering pedestrians in all directions.

The behaviour from both sides suggests that Kenyans are not keen on being controlled by signs as if they are robots, an attitude with limb and life results.

If you wish to have a garbage dump outside your house, don't start by trashing your waste.
Put up a sign saying "No dumping please."

If you wish to have a garbage dump outside your house, don't start by trashing your waste there. Put up a sign saying, "No Dumping Please". Soon you will have a mountain of garbage.

Interested in having a collage of posters on your wall in Kenya? A sign saying, "Posters Prohibited", will do the trick.

The grass grows greener where there is no sign saying, "Keep Off the Grass" while "Don't Feed the Animals" elicits insatiable curiosity on why they should not be fed.

A popular bar in Nairobi city has a huge mural of a buxom lady dancing above the jukebox. Underneath it is a sign saying, "No Dancing on the Floor." That mural is incitement enough to provoke dancing but that is normally not what motivates dancing where it is prohibited in bars.

The mere sign warning against dancing kicks legs into action.

"No Stopping for Buses and Matatu", is an open invitation for the same to do exactly that while "No Hooting", might be taken to mean, "Hoot to find out what will happen".

"Don't Drink and Drive" has already been proved in Kenya to be a national cliche whose more realistic version is "Let us have one for the road", meaning, "let us have a party before we hit the road".

Signs are sometimes respected when the consequences are immediate and dire. Only the suicidal would ignore a sign in a Nairobi bar saying, "Don't run in the bar".

The bar is located near a bus depot where pick-pocketing is a thriving business. When the pickpockets are on the run, they dash through the busy bar risking apprehension by members of the public and possible lynching.

An innocent sprinter hurrying about his business risks the same fate.

A "No weapon in the bar" warning loses its cutting edge when a Maasai or any other pastoralist, who assumes carrying a club is part of his traditional heritage and is apparently allowed to do so by the law, walks in with such a weapon. There is normally not a whimper when he puts his lethal weapon on the table and orders a beer.

There isn't a whimper either when a hawker walks into the same bar loaded with his wares which include footlong screw-drivers, a saw, a hammer and other things that are technically weapons.

Even when a customer buys one of them, it is still considered to be outside the realm of weapons until they are actually used for assault.

Dear God

That open-air garage mechanic who sometimes gives wrong diagnoses and prescriptions for my car's problems even though he claims to be an expert on all models on Kenyan roads is plain Onyango to me. He is just that man wearing greasy overalls whom I really don't trust with my car because I suspect that he might fix an old part and claim that it is brand new as is the practice among his lot. But come Sunday and the Bishop of Cantebury does not step out in the kind of splendour that Onyango does. The Pope does not inspire as much awe as that greasy mechanic when the faithful appear at his garage.

The man who is plain Onyango to me is Archbishop Alfaxed Nehemia Onyango on Sundays when the faithful of his Roho African Church of Saved Souls (RACOSS) come to his garage for spiritual dispensation or to just pay homage to one of their primates.

I don't know how Onyango reached such spiritual heights and how each Sunday or any time he is called upon to, he transforms himself from the man who calls "Hey you, bastard" to his spanner boys, to one who says "My brethren in Christ" to the congregation.

The first time I saw that transformation, Onyango was getting short-tempered with me and my car because he had worked on its overheating problem for half a day without success. His face was like an ugly smudge with frustration and anger as he bent into the bonnet. He was calling the heating system of my car all kinds of names including, "you bloody gasket", for "gasket" seems to be his popular insult for anything or anybody who refuses to bend to his mind and muscles.

Then from a distance appeared people dressed like the pictures of the Maggi, the people who went to see the child Jesus in Bethlehem, whose pictures I had seen in Bible story books when I was a child. On their heads were turbans that made them look like sheikhs. The men had the overflowing beards that the same children's books gave to Moses of the Exodus odyssey.

It was as if I was actually seeing a picture of the Old Testament prophets walking out of that picture book for the men and women in the approaching group wore flowing, brightly coloured robes. Each one of them had a huge crucifix around the neck while two people in the group were literally carrying crosses, for in their hands were long staffs with a cross on top, more like bishopric spectres but made of wood and heavier.

As they approached, the hymn they were humming reached the ears of Onyango and he looked up. Then his face changed from an oily smudge into a radiance of smiles. Saul must have undergone that kind of transformation which turned him into Paul on his way to Damascus.

He hastily wiped his oily hands to face the people who had just come from my childhood Bible stories picture book. He stretched his right hand forward with the palm open and stretched himself to his full height. He said something unintelligible in his language in a voice that befits the Pope and the faithful fell on their bellies, as if struck by some sudden and severe affliction.

He said something else and they chanted back as they rose. Onyango then touched their heads individually and as he did so, each of them seemed to have been touched by an electric current. With each touch on the head, the faithful shook violently and said something between clenched teeth. The group then moved some distance away where they held counsel with Onyango. Onyango returned to work on my car and, after explaining that he was wanted later in the evening to officiate at a funeral wake for a late RACOSS member, changed his face back to the earlier smudge.

Some days later, I wished Onyango could show the same inspiration in repairing my car as he was exhibiting as he told a RACOSS congregation under a tree, which I learned is their only place of worship: "God came to me in a dream and said, 'Alfaxed, my people have turned away from me. Go forth and awaken them from the dream that the great deceiver, the devil, has put them into. Tell them that I, Jehovah, has appointed you as my messenger to bring them back into righteousness.' From that day, I have been proclaiming His word as it was given to our forefathers in the old book of the Bible. I am his messenger and he tells you through me to repent before the diseases of sin consume you all."

Onyango, like others who challenge the supremacy of the Pope and the Bishop of Cantebury in the winning of souls, is part of home-grown religion in Kenya. He is among many others who since the 1920s have made the tree shade the church building, and appointed the bishop from the ranks of cooks. The "anointed ones" of such sects and their following would make St. Paul revise his assertion that Romans were unscrupulously religious, for Kenyans worship with such zeal and variety that church-going, meaning being at a place of worship, is as fashionable as sinning.

Such is the variety that I won't be suprised if Onyango's wife belongs to another religious sect and which, unlike the one led by her husband, decrees against worshipping on Sundays. Perhaps her sect, which is led by Onyango's neighbour, worships on Mondays and prohibits any manual labour on that day, including cooking.

The couple's first born may be a born-again Christian who goes to the huge church on Sundays where the preacher comes dressed in a three-piece suit.

It should not suprise anybody that Onyango's daughter belongs to yet another sect which prohibits the sharing of cooking pots in a home, although she lives with her family. That means that the devil is likely to stir some trouble at times because the idea of a child cooking for herself and eating as the parents watch is not the most Christian practice in Kenyan households.

Divine intervention is not always sought whenever the devil stirs a bit of trouble here and there. The devil particularly likes bringing about indecision about who is the "anointed one" to lead this and that sect and God seemingly takes to the ring side as machetes are rattled; stones whizz above the heads of the congregation; veterans of the war of liberation in Kenya throw punches; clerics in collars fly through windows and other forms of combat gain full force in the very house of prayer.

The gods of war so inspire the combatants that a man carries his Bible with as much care as the sledge hammer that is inside his coat for the latter is more likely to be more handy in case of Cain rising against Abel than the former.

Archbishop Onyango's sect, like many others, marches to the rythm of the drum not much unlike the Salvation Army. There is no brass band but there are two or so followers with throbbing drums at the head of the column of worshippers who take to the road in their flowing robes on Sunday.

Also ahead is a person carrying a flag bearing the colours of the sect, often red or green with a white strip. The flag bearer also serves as the traffic marshall, signalling vehicles to keep to the middle of the road and stopping them to let the congregation cross the road if need be.

The throbbing drums give rhythm to slow jogging steps which is a rather daunting task as the congregation is attired in those Sheikh turbans, crucifixes that dominate the chest, others in the hands, flowing robes and many times the sun is hot. That does not dampen the spirit of worship and Onyango's people will jog for many kilometres to the appointed place of worship which is almost invariably under a tree.

Such inspiration to drum becomes ungodly when it is nocturnal which is not unusual. Perhaps there is a funeral wake or it is just that a congregation inside a house is so mad with the devil that they wish to chase him away with noise. That calls for the taking of the loudest drum at that time of the night, when even the devil has taken a rest, and drumming it for hours. That noise perhaps does not wake up the devil but keeps the neighbours of the worshippers fully wake.

When Onyango goes out of his house, perhaps after a night of hard drumming, he might find a poster pasted on the electric post of his gate. It will announce the visit to the city of a foreign evangelist claiming to do more than the man of the drum does. He will claim to do such miracles to help raise the dead, make the lame walk and the blind to see. That will make Onyango wonder if Jesus himself is coming to give an encore of his deeds while he was on earth.

Even if Jesus came back today, he would find it very hard to have himself heard in Nairobi's Jeevanjee Gardens, a public park where the effort to make voices reach heaven drowns the city traffic during lunch hour. It is there that Nairobians who have no food for the stomach often look for food for the soul and find it in plenty and in variety.

At one corner of the park is a man who looks dressed for crooning in a cabaret show. He has well-groomed sideburns and his hair sits on his head as if he just took it from the hair dresser and placed it there. He dons a well-cut wollen suit in the heat of January. His tie matches the breast pocket cloth and he holds the microphone as if he is about to do an Elvis Presely act. His rich baritone is controlled.

He is saying that he saw Jesus in a nightclub where he used to commit all sorts of sins "including playing the devil's music". Amid rich intonations of "Halleluya! Praise the Lord!" he also says that had he not seen Jesus on that night when he was seeing five people instead of one because of the bhang that he had taken, he would perhaps have died of Aids for "all the women in the nightclub were mine!"

A short distance from him there are two men dressed like him who are playing guitars, backing up three women singing Skeeter Davis' "What a Friend we have in Jesus". They stop singing and one of them takes the microphone to say that she can see a river of the blood of Jesus coming to clean those sinners in the park including those "who at that moment are more concerned about eating their chips in groups rather than listen to the good word".

At the centre of the park, is turbaned and barefoot Chege, who unlike the other preachers does not have a public address system. A Bible lies at his feet and he hardly refers to it during the one hour preaching session. However, what he loses in Biblical references is compensated for by his ability to get to the heart of the matter by telling it as it is. He promises no fire or brimstone but pain where it matters most, for he is telling the predominantly male audience that women are like "atomic bombs which explode and leave you in pieces".

Most of the men nod but others quietly creep away when he says, "I challenge you that if you agreed to be medically examined at this moment, some of you are suffering from afflictions passed on to you by women." No man challenges him that some of the men might have passed on the afflictions to many women.

Moving violations

Whenever I look at my car and I am in a mood to absorb guilt, I think of the film, "Moving Violations." When I look at many other cars actually moving on the road, I see moving violations. When I get into public transport vehicles, I see such other violations. But all these violations provide the means of getting here and there barring almost certain breakdowns, certain arrests by the police and invariably easy-to-pay court fines for violating a good part of the highway code.

The unconscious and sometimes almost conscious aim of these violations is to cause interminable loss of life and limb. That is so because those violations move from place to place when they should be immobile. A car that has tyres as smooth as the "tongue of a snake" as it is said, and which rattles as if it has been seized by convulsions, is safer standing still than moving. But such cars in Kenya are driven by such a strong urge to be on the road that they would rather be on the move.

They are at times double moving violations because the driver is also a violation for one reason or other. In some instances the driver has never done a driving test, yet he drives a public taxi with a sticker above his seat reading, "Don't panic. Expert driver in control". The same driver might be the type that considers going behind the wheel when he cannot see straight. He prefers to drive when he is seeing double under the influence of what he has drank or smoked.

The guilt that I feel for owning a moving violation is sometimes washed off by the fact that I own "wheels" as a car of any description is called. It is a sign that I have "arrived" unlike those pedestrians who haven't and don't only have to put up with the rigours of walking but also run the risk of being run over on the pavement by a moving violation and certainly being splashed with a mud bath when it rains.

Having so arrived, I must announce that fact, a thing that I do by swinging the keys of my car in my hand whenever there is an audience. That is why I must be excused for dropping the keys on the table in a bar or restaurant when there are other people there. That is why the keys must have a holder that announces a car model. No Volkswagen keyholders please. The holder must announce that it is nothing short of a Toyota.

Saddam Hussein for all the bad names that he got in the Gulf War, was a good ally in my efforts to say that I belong to the class of those who have arrived by owning "wheels". "This Gulf crisis," I would announce with the gravity of a sheikh who has lost an oil well to a B-52 bomber, "has hurt us motorists. If I did not own a Toyota, a car with a low fuel consumption, I don't know how I would have survived the daily budget."

In the privacy of that car, I have my own worries about being on the road, one of them being that I might meet a traffic policeman who is not open to such reasons as, "I cannot fit new tyres because I cannot afford them". I am also worried about the driver ahead of me. His passenger is a lady who is knitting a sweater profusely. Her lips are tightly shut to emphasise the fact that the man beside her is her husband and that they are not on talking terms. The man is averse to silence and is mumbling to himself, letting one hand go off the steering to make an angry gesture at no one and nothing specific.

The lights refuse to respond to his honking and stay red.

79

The lights turn red and he stops with a screech, interrupting the knitting that is going on beside him. The driver gives the red lights an angry stare and then honks although there is nobody ahead of him at the lights. The lights refuse to respond to his honking and stay red. He taps his steering wheel in an irritated manner and honks again, this time more loudly while looking at the lights with a snarl on his face.

The lights don't change. His hand stays on the horn, blaring at the lights until time comes for them to change and he takes off, leaving behind the smell of burning rubber.

Somebody honks from behind and when I look at my rear-view mirror, which I have patched with masking tape lest it falls off, I see a driver menacingly driving right behind me as if to push me into movement now that my car is not capable of shooting off as soon as the lights turn amber. I honk and make a rude gesture at him in the spirit of the national occupation of drivers: honking when it is not necessary.

Drivers honk when they see a chicken ahead and not when a woman, so loaded with things on her back that her ears are muffled, crosses ahead of them. They honk when other cars stall ahead of them and not when, approaching a bend where there are likely to be children. They honk to greet their friends who are also furiously honking back on almost empty highways and not in crowded residential estates where children are playing with rag balls. They honk to show off their musical horns and not when the car ahead of them is about to cross into the next lane carelessly. They honk in hospital yards, as they flash past a bad accident where their help is needed and not when they should be doing so to alert the other driver that he has a flat tyre.

There are also drivers who don't honk whether it is necessary or, not. They don't because their car horns don't work at all.

Honk if you are Kenyan but if you cannot, then flash your lights, but never put on your headlights until it is pitch dark. Flash to warn the oncoming driver that there is a police check where he is going. Flash to warn him that soccer fans are stoning cars ahead and to tell him that if he does not slow down he will be trapped by the police radar hidden at the corner. Flash your lights to tell the driver ahead of you that his car is too slow and that you want to overtake. Flash to tell the pedestrians crossing the road at the zebra crossing that if they don't clear out in a flash you will run the whole lot of them down.

Flash to say that you are driving like you are mad because you have recently bought the car and you want to show off. Flash your lights to announce that you are drunk and incapable of handling a car.

For double effect, some drivers combine angry honking with incessant flashing of lights. I faced that when I was learning how to drive as the car tended to stall, frustrating my efforts to balance the clutch pedal and the accelerator. I faced much more, for apart from the flashing, the driver shouted through his window, "get off the road you woman!" I understood that to mean that only women are daft enough not to know how to drive. That driver hadn't met the kind of woman I saw one day. She was driving a moving violation like many of us, and it stalled. The driver behind her honked and flashed his lights but that would not make the car ahead move. The woman was meanwhile pumping the accelerator pedal furiously hoping to coax her car into life. The more she pumped fuel without making the car move, the more the honking and flashing of lights behind.

Then the woman got out of her car and matched to the honking driver. She handed him her keys and told him to go ahead and start the stalled car if he thought he was a miracle-worker. After that he found sense in the fact that he could drive around the stalled car and get to where he was going.

Speed limits and traffic lights are generally considered a nuisance by many drivers as they impede the movement of moving violations from place to place. That is, amber before the lights turn red, in Kenya means pass on and amber before green means shoot ahead and honk angrily if the driver ahead of you is not moving. That is why red at traffic lights means go ahead if there is no policemen nearby, even if you are likely to collide with the car coming from the opposite direction.

The inconvenience of being stopped by speed control policemen is minimised, if not totally eliminated, by the use of flashing lights and well-choreographed use of the right hand. It is bad manners for any motorist to let a fellow driver be caught at a speed control check if his lights are working.

After you have passed a speed radar without a speeding ticket because another driver had warned you of the danger, you look out for oncoming drivers. Once you see one, you flash your lights and then stretch out your right hand outside the window. Flag it up and down as if giving a stopping sign. Then point your finger to the

81

ground repeatedly in a way that suggests that the motorist you are warning is driving on an explosive mine. That driver will automatically slow down, put on the face of a bishop until he passes the police radar then resume speeding as if in a motoring rally.

If you want to know what danger in the form of the police lies ahead, flash your lights without making any hand gestures. The oncoming driver will certainly give you the appropriate response, including a thumbs up one indicating that there is no danger of meeting the police.

There are of course, other signs of danger ahead apart from flashing lights and flagging hands. Such signs are seen on weekends and on public holidays. One example is an oncoming car that is taking most of the road at the speed of a rocket. The car's stereo is blaring, the driver is trying to kiss his equally jolly passenger while behind them are three goggle-eyed fellows singing along with the car's stereo. The wise thing to do is give way as there is a chance that you and the occupants of the other car are likely to be the subject of yet another item in the newspaper saying, "six more die on the road," as that kind of news is so regular that a spot seems to be permanently allocated to it.

There is a commonly accepted opinion among many drivers that vision is improved by alcohol and hence the popular call for a round, "Let's have one for the road." One for the road is often a modest way of saying, let's get drunk and then drive off. The definition of drunken driving is that a driver caused an accident and was arrested – and not that he had excessive alcohol in his blood system while driving. That is why my friend Alcoholycus Anonymus would feel very insulted if you suggested that he cannot drive even when he cannot stand on one leg due to the influence of alcohol.

Mr Anonymus drinks Tusker Lager and does not consider himself ready to go home until he has drank enough to pronounce Tusker, "Tashika." With so many bottles of "Tashika" in his system, he is half deaf, half blind and nearly totally lame. He is almost deaf because if you suggest that you go home, he responds with a nod and says, "Yesh, another Tashika for me,"and he asks for it menacingly.

The beer is delivered and because he is half blind, his hand reaches for a full glass belonging to somebody else and not his that needs to be refilled. He drowns the contents of the stranger's glass and then noisily asks what happened to the beer that he had ordered which, in the meantime, is standing infront of him.

The eyes of Mr Anonymous are drowsy and threatening to close but we dare not let him doze off as we are depending on his car to get us home. We raise him up and he grumbles about men like us who go home early because they are afraid of being beaten by their wives. We ignore the slur and half carry and half drag the man to the car.

Once out on the street, he leans on his car fumbling for his car keys. It takes three minutes for him to get them and two more to put the key into the ignition hole. One of us offers to drive the car home and that gives instant speech power to its owner.

"What do you mean? Drive my car? Over my dead body! I cannot trash anybody witch my car, okay? I cannot risk having my car wrecked by anybody so I drive you guys home if you want to go." He slumps into the driver's seat. The car zigzags out of the parking lot, its tail lights drawing meandering patterns in the night.

If the driver survives his escapade, this will be material for heroic accounts. "Say what," he will tell his friends the following day while having a beer to presumably cure a hangover. "I don't know how I got home. I had quite a bit to drink last night. I remember getting into the car but I don't know who drove it home. I guess my car knows its way home."

It was the same Alcoholycus Anonymous who read in the newspaper the proposed introduction of breathalysers in Kenya. He was among the people who were heard speaking in whispers as if they were discussing news of an invasion by aliens from space, the introduction of what was to be an enormously unpopular gadget called alcohometer. They talked with horror about the accuracy of the gadget in assessing the quantity of alcohol in a driver's blood. There were broad smiles when the dreaded gadget was not introduced.

Alcoholycus Anonymous will not pause to think if you offer him one for the road because the best that the police can do is smell his breath to test whether or not he has been drinking. He knows that however good a sniffer a policeman is, he has no chance of knowing how much a driver has drank. Only a urine or blood test is likely to bring results and Alcoholycus Anonymous knows that it is not too often that a driver gets tested for that...well, not until he or she has caused an accident.

Signs of the times

With so many experts claiming that they live in Kenya, I don't see why anything should go wrong. But many things go wrong, including my car which has a chronic overheating problem despite being repaired over and over again by a mechanic who claims to be an expert.

The signboard outside his open-air garage screams: "Mr. Onyango and Sons Garage East Africa Ltd. Expert mechanics and panel beaters. Experts in Japanese models: Toyota, Datsun, Ford Cortina, Citroen, Isuzu, Peugeot, Kombis, etc" Next to the sign is the picture of a car, whose model is hard to make out and beneath it is a picture of a man, presumably Onyango, minus his son, with a load of spanners beside him.

I don't know when a Ford Cortina became a Japanese model and even if such a model's engine was a Greek one to Onyango, he calls himself an expert because next door is Mutiso, the tree shade barber who is also an expert. Above the huge cracked customer's mirror is a sign written on cardboard paper saying, "Mutiso, son of Nguli expat Bamba". He did not write the sign for his spelling teacher and some of his customers must wonder what it all means as they can't read at all. If they can't read, they can look at the drawings of the heads displayed beneath the sign showing the hair cuts that Mutiso the expert is capable of.

There is a crew cut, a hair cut resembling Eddy Murphy's, an Isaac Hayes clean shave, a cut that resembles the crest of a cock, and a cut that does not look a cut at all since the head seems to have lost its hair long ago.

I have seen similar drawings in barber shops, no doubt the work of an artist. Most of the people who are worked on by Mutiso's hair clippers seem to prefer the cock crest style for that is what they walk away with. I am more inclined to think that he is not capable of any other style but he retains the claim of being an expert.

Onyango owns the garage with his sons because that is the natural thing in Kenya. I have yet to see a business with the name, "So and So and daughters". It seems as if it is against good business sense to say that a daughter has a hand in it.

Perhaps that is why Barnabas, the old shopkeeper back at the village, invented the claim that he brazenly displayed on top of his shop that he was the father of sons who jointly owned the business with him when his only son had died at infancy to leave him the father of daughters who had no interest at all in buying and selling.

Onyango has sons alright, and one of them helps him out at the garage, but I am not sure about joint ownership with that fellow or any other that he has brought into this world. Whenever I take my car there, he always says something to the effect that "my garage is this and that."

It is a limited company only because he is the sole shareholder, sole managing director, chief mechanic and leading expert, chief cashier, personnel officer, only salesman and auditor. The claim of the garage having wings all over East Africa might be Onyango's designs to have fame in the region. As of now, he is quite famous for not being an expert in anything other than pulling out spark plugs and polishing them, only to later claim, "the car's exhaust pipe is weeping water instead of smoke", that is, "it is tuned better than ever before".

We pay Onyango well because we believe that since he claims to be an expert, he is one. So he has saved some of the money and opened a hair "salon" for his wife. A "salon" it is, for that is what anybody who owns a hair treatment concern for women calls it. There are no bat wings, sharp-shooting behind and under the arm without looking, and Texan drawls as horses lie in wait, tethered outside for the master's quick escape in our salons.

There is plenty of hair-sizzling, experiences too womanly to be found in a salon.

They are not exactly the hair-raising experiences one would find inside "Space Challenger". This vessel was made in Japan originally as an Isuzu bus just about the same time the Americans were launching one with a similar name in space. The terrestial and aerial variety of "Space Challenger" don't share the same speed. But this is not to say that the driver will not try to fly, particularly while "Desert Storm" is ahead picking up passengers which the driver of "Space Challenger" thinks belong to his vehicle. "Desert Storm", having been in existence with Saddam Hussein, stands all the chances of picking up most passengers and killing them as it takes a corner like a space shuttle that has suddenly lost its ground command.

"Apollo Eleven-Murang'a Express" makes no pretences at flying; for crawling along is a problem as it belongs to the "Apollo 11" spacecraft vintage. It is popular with old folks who are not in an express hurry to fly to their Maker before they get to their destination: Murang'a.

"Apollo Eleven-Murang'a Express" makes no claim to attempted flights, but it has its own pretensions. Its name suggests seriousness in getting passengers to their destination non-stop.

It is a pretension that the passengers seem to be part of as nobody complains when the bus stops twenty times during the 70-kilometre journey. None of them says a word when it reverses for half a kilometre to pick up a sack that had fallen off its roof rack. Nobody says a thing when it stops at a bus stop where there is no waiting passenger as the conductor stands on raised ground, shields his eyes with his open palm as he looks for passengers in the horizon and then starts chewing a piece of sugarcane as the driver opens the flap covering the engine beside him.

The sons and daughters of the old folks who are dozing in "Apollo Eleven-Murang'a Express" are in "Lady Diana", the mini bus that has just flashed by. Behind it is "Star Dust", a vehicle of similar make. Their next stop is Thika where the drivers will cool off at "Thika International Cafe". It has never been heard of out of the town but perhaps its owner calls it so because the menu card says that it offers "international menu".

Most people there, however, prefer to go for humble things such as "sosange" and "sips" so spelt in the menu. There is no surprise in those kinds of items on the menu for they are just humble sausages and chips. Spread some "tomato source" on them and you have a meal. Perhaps it is "tomato source" because once, it was tomato sauce, then the cafe's proprietor in his wisdom decided to spread its application over more plates than intended and, as usual in many such cases diluted it. The plastic bottle in which it is contained was indeed once the source of real sauce.

If you want your imagination to take a flight alongside that of the cafe's proprietor, ask for items that sound more exotic than "sosange and sips". The menu, obviously copied from another of nobler tastes, will feature such items as "chicken marengo". That is boiled chicken dipped in fat.

And talking of offers, I never take notice of a bookshop that claims to sell "stationary". And there are many that offer such goods. I ignore that kind of sign as I do others that say don't do this and that because it is totally incomprehensible how a person can obey a sign that is very well posted.

You might be, for instance, considered rather eccentric if you ignore that red sign on public buses in the city that says, *"Usisimame kwa mlango"* (Don't stand at the door). Once you see that kind of sign, move to the door even if the bus is half-empty. It is even more fashionable to do so if you have luggage in one hand.

Once you are the closest that you can get to stepping out of the bus, hold the hand rail and stick your head outside with your bus ticket clenched between your teeth ready for inspection by the conductor. Meanwhile, as you try to get most of your body outside, hold your luggage in the other hand. When the conductor comes and warns you that you will fall, pretend that he is asking you for the ticket which is clenched between your teeth. Shake your head vigorously to say that you cannot manage to take out the ticket from your mouth and give it to him as both your hands are occupied.

87

Continue riding that way until the bus is about to stop at your destination. Jump off the bus just before the driver steps on the brakes.

The hanging-out heroics are achieved even better when the bus is full. Wait at a bus stop and let all buses that have no passengers standing at the door pass. Once you see one in which there are people who are as daring as you – for that is what you think you are, not foolish – already hanging at the door, join them. Hold on to somebody's coat if there is nowhere to hold on to and arch your body as if you are part of an open umbrella. Watch the ground whizz by as if you are totally outside the bus. This has a double advantage in that you can show off your heroics and at the same time avoid paying your bus fare as the conductor cannot reach you.

Only a masochist will take the sign, *"usicheze dansi hapa"*, ("No dancing") posted above a juke box seriously. That is an invitation to dance whenever somebody has fed the machine with money, for you don't have to do it from your own pocket. Do a bull dance and nobody will mind but soon, you might find another man wanting to dance with you. There is nothing beyond it but a man wanting to get the

worth of the shilling that has been put in juke box, for what is music for if not to be danced to?

There is a sign that you might ignore at your peril if you are a real stranger in Nairobi. The sign is *"Mbwa Kali"* and is posted on most gates in plush residential areas. Its regularity gives the impression that *"Mbwa Kali"* is as popular a name as "Smith" until you want to go in to enquire into the health of a particular *"Mbwa Kali"*, particularly if you just walk to the gate and open it. The welcome will most likely be torn pants or torn buttocks, the work of a well-fed Alsatian who will answer to the name *"Mbwa Kali"*, for that just means, "fierce dog". There isn't always a terror behind the gate and the sign is put up to say that the owner of the house qualifies to have such a canine and does not have one or just to boost the morale of the dog inside, better known for its bark than its bite.

The city of strangers

Thunder and lightning did not shake us little boys growing up in the village in Central Kenya as much as they did that boy who made an annual visit there during Christmas. The fellow called himself "Born City", an emphatic label saying that he had seen none of that rustic life that made our lives because he was born in the city.

The very special thing that we noted about him with awe because we were more familiar with fist-fights that resembled badly choreographed comedies in the area of warfare, was his ability to do highly dramatised karate poses and scream louder than his Kung-Fu film mentors. The day of his departure was celebrated because the stranger among us turned a communal thing into a one-man show in warfare and that was not fair.

The stranger went back to where he was also a stranger for Nairobi has always been a city of strangers since that day when a bunch of people found a spot with cool water to wash off their sweat and dust at the head of the "Lunatic Express" as the Kenya-Uganda Railway that they were building was called. The strangers were Britons using the British tax payers' money and employing hardened labourers from India – Coolies – and their idea was not to build the future capital of Kenya.

They came upon a place that the original natives – the Maasai – who saw no need to build anything apart from their "Manyatta", called "Ewaso Nairobi", or the place of cold water, and thought it was good for a railway depot.

The locomotive sheds have since those days at the turn of the last century, turned into the home of strangers attracted to it by its virtues and vices. They are there to work, trade wares and body, beg with menace and tact, steal in style or by force, visit to fleece a relative or spend money saved over the years holed in a hotel where nobody talks to the other or in one where you cannot be heard above the jukebox sound or they get married to a stranger that your mother won't look at twice, or do anything else that a stranger can do in the city.

The first strangers who lorded over the city from the days when a major issue in the council agenda was whether or not to buy a refuse collection donkey, were representatives of Her Majesty's Government in Britain and, in their inspiration, they called it "The City in the

Sun". Plenty of sun still shines over the city only to be cut off by the skyscrapers that compete to reach the sky.

Native strangers now lord over it as city fathers, owners of shopping complexes where you can get "masala" ground in India but miss maize flour ground in Kenya from Kenyan maize.

The strangers still refuse to call Nairobi home even when they own fortified castles where they live under the protection of bull dogs and emaciated watchmen. They will call that mansion a house and that hut in the rural area home. A grass thatched hut, a hasty assembly of blocks and corrugated iron sheets, an architectural marvel that blends Gothic and modern columns in the rural area, is a home but not that castle with a heated swimming pool in Nairobi.

The stranger at times has a very strange relationship with "home". He takes a loan from the co-operative society where he works to build a "home". Meanwhile, he is still "eating ugali with salt" as they say of a person when he does not have enough to eat because he is paying a mortgage for a house in Nairobi.

He lives in the "house" for 360 days and sleeps in the "home" for five days: On Christmas day, New Year's Day, Easter Sunday and one other public holiday. He might spend another night there when he goes to the funeral of a friend in the rural area.

He might not even sleep in that "home" at all for a single day although the mansion stands like an anthill among those mud-walled huts of peasants. The man goes to the rural area five times a year alright, but does not step in the mansion. The stranger in the city where he might have gone after secondary school education might be the type that fears the "evil eye" in the rural area, which has been accused of "arresting" a person's efforts to become rich.

In that case, "home" is the best hotel in town. That won't stop the man from saying, when he gets back to the city, "I have just come from home and the people greet you."

I built a "home", an architectual design that does not allow windows to open properly because the edges of the roof drop too low, long ago when I did not have enough money to construct something better because I feared bad words would follow me to my grave in case I died before I had built a "home". Considering that, like a good Kenyan, I wanted to be buried at "home", I built that "home" to rest when the time comes to be said of me, "soil shall return to the soil". Nobody makes a negative verbal post-mortem that says how distant I was from home.

I have heard it said at a funeral, while tears flowed, perhaps more of out pity that the deceased had no home than that he had departed: "What! This man did not have a home here? Unbelievable."

"I too, would not have thought that it would be so," sobs another mourner. "He had a big mansion in the city. He could have at least built something small out here. Even a shed of sorts could have been better than this emptiness."

For the strangers from Europe, America, and Asia, Nairobi could be home, for a person is always either trying to pretend to make it so or actually doing so. That is why a hotel will claim to cook Ukranian food the way your mother used to. The only difference between what your mother used to make and what you get is that it will be served by a waiter looking like a clown who has run away from a circus as he dresses in attire that he claims represents a typical Ukranian.

Hare Krishna ceased to be a stranger in Nairobi long ago and his name is chanted by strangers to the city, who happen to be Africans, who the other day were worshipping a god who lived on a mountain. Kenyans who some years ago swore by their next piece of meat, stand on their heads in meditation while being nourished by vegeterian diets of strange believers.

Strangers from Europe and America no longer have exclusive rights to teach Kenyan strangers in Nairobi bad habits. The African strangers have enough of those. One of them is chewing "miraa" and then spitting the green glob from the chewed twigs at the feet of the person sitting next to you in a restaurant.

Some strangers from Europe seem to take to that habit quite easily and also to that one of banging the table in a bar if service is not forthcoming.

While the Croatian will go to that food festival that promises him a menu that will remind him why he is not a Serbian, I will go to that bar owned by "man from home" when I don't want to feel like a stranger in the city. The place owned by "man from home" is where people from my village go when they want to know the latest news from home, for that is where those who have been "home", meaning the village, more recently, bring the news. That is also where life and death are discussed.

When a man from "home" working in the city dies, we meet at "the place of the man from home" to make funeral plans so that the deceased can be transported home. When a young man from home wants to marry, we meet at "the place of the man from home" to plan the wedding that will take place at "home" although that is two hundred kilometres away. When a man from home has been promoted at work, we toast his success at "the place of the man from home". We all feel good to spend money on beer at "the place of the man from home" as his prosperity is also ours, we say.

My aunt has many things to hand over to me to give to the strangers in the city whenever I go home. One of them is plenty of greetings for all the people from the village who are there because she imagines that it is a small village where everybody sees everybody else.

She gives me a load of greetings to give the "daughter of Hezekia" who is in the city although I have not seen her since the day she became a Muslim and stopped going to "the place of the man from home". "Take this bunch of bananas to her and tell her that I pray for her regularly," my aunt tells me as she puts yet another gift into my car for some stranger in the city. I begin worrying about where I will get the "daughter of Hezekia" because I don't know where she lives or works although she comes from "home". I dare not tell auntie that lest she accuses me of abandoning "people from home" in the city.

As she hands over a rooster to me as my final gift, I have forgotten about the "daughter of Hezekia" but Auntie brings the memory of the lost one back. "Don't keep the bananas of the daughter of Hezekia for too long before handing them to her lest they go bad," she cautions.

As I drive back to the city, the load of arrow roots in the boot of my car starts to seem strange in the city. It does not blend with the ambience that is literally wafting from Muthaiga I, the residence of the British High Commissioner to Kenya where the Queen's Birthday Party is in progress. Africans who are strangers to the city and to the celebration of birthdays of monarchs are streaming into the residence, trying to graft an air of being familiar with such functions on their true selves.

That top civil servant who would be more comfortable at his version of "the place of the man from home" is stifled in a woolen three-piece suit and tagging on his arm as she has seen on films featuring the gentry, is his wife. She looks as if she is wearing the behind of an ostrich on her head as her hat is rather richly decorated with gay feathers. Behind them is a man in a kilt nostalgically carrying part of "back home" with him to the party. Most likely, a bemedalled veteran of the Second World War will be trying to relive the jungles of Burma as if there never was Baghdad and Saddam Hussein.

My mind is busy puzzling out how to get the "daughter of Hezekiah" now that I am joining the city centre traffic but she is put out of my mind by the honking of a London-look taxi, yet another stranger in Nairobi. There are two strangers in it: the African driver who came from the rural areas to make a living, and an Asian customer, perhaps a grandson of the "Lunatic Express" builders. He is chewing a strange thing in Nairobi; the triangular "kauli pan". Perhaps it reminds him of home - India - where he has never been.

As I give the taxi way, I nearly knock down a Kenyan who is perhaps a total stranger in Nairobi. He is wearing a strange thing; a T-shirt with the inscription, "Save Lake Ontario". I wonder whether he is mumbling "save Nairobi" since I nearly knocked him down as he was trying to avoid a load of garbage on the roadside. Later, I notice that he is more bothered about the plastic packet in his hand holding a hamburger, perhaps bought from an establishment brought by strangers; the Wimpy cafés.

I am in the City Centre which is bisected by two main thoroughfares: Kenyatta Avenue, named after Kenya's first president and Moi Avenue, named after his successor. Other main roads, avenues, streets and lanes in Nairobi are named after living politicians and I wonder why, since political life is such a fragile thing in Kenya.

Life in the City Centre for me begins and ends east of Moi Avenue in the location of River Road. It is true that you can lose your life there and the joke is that you can buy anything there, including a brand new soul, which is to say, anything goes. New life begins there as the rest of the city goes to sleep.

When night falls on that part of town called "the town below River Road", a watchman who looks as if he was brought to his place of work on a wheelchair slips on an overcoat proudly announcing that he works for "Scuds Security Company". He lights, a charcoal fire in the metal cover of a City Council dustbin. He is soon dozing off, the unfinished maize cob he has been eating still in his hand.

A woman comes by and it is easy to tell that she is a prostitute. As she passes by the lamp post, the cake of rouge on her face, the walk that says "take me or leave me", accentuated by a yoyo-like swaying of the hips, jeans that clamp her buttocks like a vice and the clap-clap of her shoes, say she is out on business.

She stops, opens her handbag and out comes a cigarette stub. Apparently, times are not very good and a cigarette must be stubbed out to be smoked later. The moment has arrived.

As she bends to pick up a splinter from the watchman's fire, the sleeping figure suddenly comes to life, *rungu* in hand ready to strike. On seeing who it is that has disturbed his sleep, the "Scuds Security" figure goes back to sleep with a smile.

It is a cold night and it looks like it is going to be even colder for the girl who has now squatted near the fire as is usual during the lean days of the month when there is little of that "If you have the money dear, I have the time to spare".

The girl should have been in the place of the watchman because her eyes can see in the dark and her ears hear the footsteps of death. She hears a sound and looks over her shoulder and sees three shadows in long coats and the fourth with long ears and walking on fours. It is the police and she takes off her high heeled shoes, ready to creep away. The police and their canine companion are however too quick.

She puts on the face of a rural girl who has just come to the city and claims the watchman, who has now woken up and is looking like a lamp post which has been knocked by a car, stands at attention, is her uncle. The watchman nods but the policemen have other ideas about where the girl should be at that hour.

Even the police dog looks credulous about this sanguineous relationship between the girl and the watchman and sits on its haunches looking bored. It springs back to life in apparent agreement with its master when the girl fishes out twenty shillings from her bag and gives it to the policemen, saying that it is a cold night and that they need tea. As the policemen walk away, girl and uncle part ways without a word to each other. They are just two strangers in the city meeting on a cold night and expecting strange happenings.

Two blocks down the street, somebody is belting out a song, having come from a local liquor bar. His hollering does not seem strange in the dead of the night. The girl who has just parted with twenty shillings spits when she sees the drunk. She thinks he is detestable. As he walks towards the direction of the policemen, he won't find it strange to be asked for twenty shillings by them, or risk sleeping in the cells. It is likely that he will also meet another stranger who has had nothing to eat and drink who will demand that he hands over what he has in his pockets. He will not find that strange on River Road.

Fixed price

There is a notice that my wife always ignores like many other Kenyans: "Fixed price" prominently displayed in a shop. She thinks that it is put up for gullible people like me and should be ignored all the time. She is a hard bargainer and no amount of persuasion through such signs and nudging on the behind while shopping will stop her from trying to bring the price of an item down.

Many times she scores a point with that bargaining despite the time spent on it. She does so by making the shop attendant look like a liar by devaluing the item on sale to the lowest price that she can reach.

"What do you mean," she says, almost with a sneer as she holds the silk scarf high, "this is the same type of scarf that I saw in the shop five blocks away selling for half this price."

The shop attendant tells her to go and buy it there if the price is so good in that other shop. My wife does not leave. Instead she looks at the scarf as if it has been collected from a dustbin although she knows that it costs more in the shop she had mentioned.

She says, "This is imitation silk made in Korea. This is not genuine silk. I can tell the genuine one when I see it."

The shop attendant shows her the label that says that the item was manufactured in China. My wife looks at the label with the same disdain that she has shown for the rest of the scarf and says, "Labels don't mean much these days. Perhaps even this thing is made in Nairobi. I will not pay more than a hundred shillings for it. That is all I have got and I won't pay a cent more."

The shop attendant reminds her once again that the shop sells goods at fixed prices. She looks at him as if to ask what language he is speaking and says once again, "One hundred shillings or nothing."

Meanwhile I am boiling inside with impatience because my wife has enough money to pay for the scarf at the fixed price. Before coming to the shop, she had checked the price and asked for the appropriate amount from me. I can do nothing at this moment to make her pay up because she is determined to pay less.

She makes as if to leave in disgust and when we take a few steps towards the door, the shop attendant calls us back saying that he is open to negotiations. Once again my wife devalues the scarf by claiming that the material is third-rate but the price first-rate.

The shop attendant in turn sings interminable praises of the scarf and its price. Finally, he concedes to a five-shilling rebate. My wife grumbles as she pays, promising never to go to that shop again.

The only places I bargain hard are where the potential customers are mostly tourists: curio shops. There, I won't hesitate to say, "I want an African's price for this bracelet."

The curio dealer will smile knowingly and say, "Certainly I will give you the price of my African customers." With that the "fixed price" will come down substantially, and even then my wife will bargain to bring it further down.

A tourist is expected to pay heaven for that "genuine elephant hair bracelet" being sold by the street hawker. The same hawker won't attempt to sell to me the same item at the price for Africans for I will be quick to remind him that unless he is a poacher or their agent, he has no business dealing with elephant hair as the hunting of jumbos was banned long ago.

Since you are a tourist expected to be carrying loads of money and very little substance in your head, the hawker will burn the edges of the plastic bracelet, push it to your nose and swear that is the smell of elephant hair that is wafting.

The hawker can spot that potential customer who is likely to confuse burning plastic with elephant hair any time. He or she normally looks like a reincarnation of Dr David Livingstone or any other 18th century explorer going into the "heart of darkness"

He or she sports a khaki pith helmet with a chin strap and shorts and bush jacket to match. Footwear is inevitably safari boots, the shoes which, the Bata marketers say, "say that you know Africa". For full effect, a hunting knife is sheathed in the belt like Tarzan set to face the jungle. All that gear has been bought in New York where the image of the jungle that awaits the visitor has been created.

So attired, the tourist walks in the streets as if he or she expects a buffalo to charge any time. He or she cannot believe that the skyscrapper is not a jungle tree that has suddenly been transformed into stone.

It is that kind of tourist who is not only easily excitable in the streets but also in the real jungle as it happened one night in a game lodge when a male buffalo gave birth.

We were sitting in the game watch platform, our eyes trained on the salt lick where a variety of game was expected to come and drink

water under a spotlight. We were getting desperate to see big game as only an antelope and a couple of warthogs had come to the watering hole when a woman who was next to me clutched her husband and said in ecstasy, "What luck, Henry! Look, a buffalo giving birth right in front of us."

I was as excited as the woman to see a buffalo in that natural process but on closer scrutiny of the approaching animal, it turned out to be only a bull with rather generous testicles.